Quick & Easy
Hexie Quilts

Dr. Peggy G. Rhodes & Julia C. Wood

American Quilter's Society

P.O. Box 3290 • Paducah, KY 42002-3290
Fax 270-898-1173 • e-mail: orders@AQSquilt.com

Located in Paducah, Kentucky, the American Quilter's Society (AQS) is dedicated to promoting the accomplishments of today's quilters. Through its publications and events, AQS strives to honor today's quiltmakers and their work and to inspire future creativity and innovation in quiltmaking.

EXECUTIVE BOOK EDITOR: ANDI MILAM REYNOLDS
BOOK EDITOR: KATHY DAVIS
GRAPHIC DESIGN: JEFFREY BECK
COVER DESIGN: MICHAEL BUCKINGHAM
QUILT PHOTOGRAPHY: CHARLES R. LYNCH

Additional copies of this book may be ordered from the American Quilter's Society, PO Box 3290, Paducah, KY 42002-3290, or online at www.AmericanQuilter.com.

Text © 2013, Authors, Dr. Peggy G. Rhodes and Julia C. Wood
Artwork © 2013, American Quilter's Society

American Quilter's Society
P.O. Box 3290 • Paducah, KY 42002-3290
Fax 270-898-1173 • e-mail: orders@AQSquilt.com

Library of Congress Control Number: 2013932283

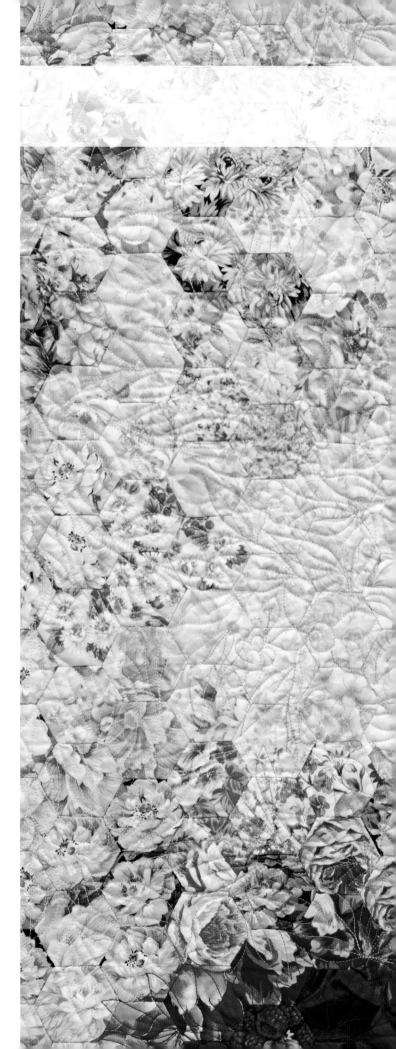

COLOR EXPLOSION, detail, full quilt on page 32.

Table of Contents (Pg. 4): HEXIE MANIA, detail, Full quilt on page 53.

Introduction (Pg. 6): MOTHER'S FLOWERS, detail, full quilt on page 62.

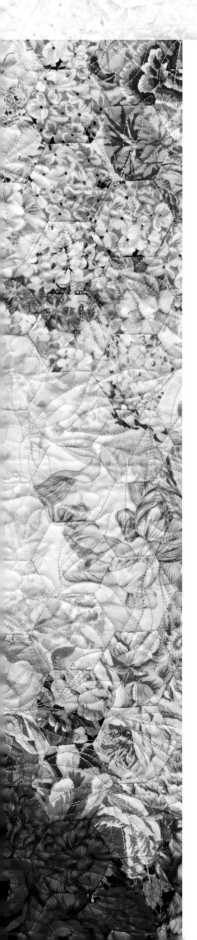

Acknowledgments

Though several similar methods of making hexagons from circles of fabric are available on the Internet, the exact method covered in this book was learned from Ozell Womack and a group of quilters from the Scottsboro Star Stitchers Guild during a Bluegrass Festival at Paint Rock Valley, Alabama, in 2008. These ladies are to be commended for sharing their time and their skills with those of us who were fortunate to have crossed their paths that day. Without them, this book truly would have never been written.

Special appreciation to our many quilting friends from the Birmingham Quilters Guild who shared our enthusiasm, encouraged us to develop the book proposal, and celebrated with us as we learned the proposal was accepted for publication. Thanks go to our quilt bees for their continued support and advice as the projects were developed—One Stitch Closer Bee and the Second Friday Bee. Special thanks also to good friends Donna Bonin who made hundreds of hexies for COLOR EXPLOSION; to Virginia Bonham who made the Rail Fence background for MOTHER'S FLOWERS (months before Peggy was ready for it) and for stitching together countless rows of hexies for COLOR EXPLOSION; to Nancy Dunavant who took time away from her retreat projects to whipstitch a row of hexies together; and to Elayne Vognild who not only did a fabulous job professionally quilting many of the quilts for this book but also pitched in and helped with binding. We also wish to thank Andi Reynolds, Executive Book Editor, and our editor, Kathy Davis, for a job well done.

AccuQuilt deserves a round of thanks for the creation of the Studio model and the numerous dies that made the production of literally thousands of circle hexies so much easier and more accurate. The Go! Baby® that you provided added portability to many of the circle-cutting needs for the book projects.

We are humbled by and eternally grateful for the many blessings we've received from our Creator—not the least of which is the ability to see His creation with a quilter's perspective.

Finally, how do you adequately thank those who literally put much of their lives on hold; graciously ate many fast food meals; didn't say a word about the undone washing and ironing; accepted the fact that we would always be accompanied by one or more hexie projects no matter where we were going; and spent hours too numerous to count alone in order to allow us to spend uninterrupted hours working on the projects and the manuscript? Such was the case with our husbands, Mark Wood and Ronald Rhodes, and Julia's daughters, Emily Wood Traylor and Elizabeth Wood. We sincerely hope each of you know just how appreciated and loved you are.

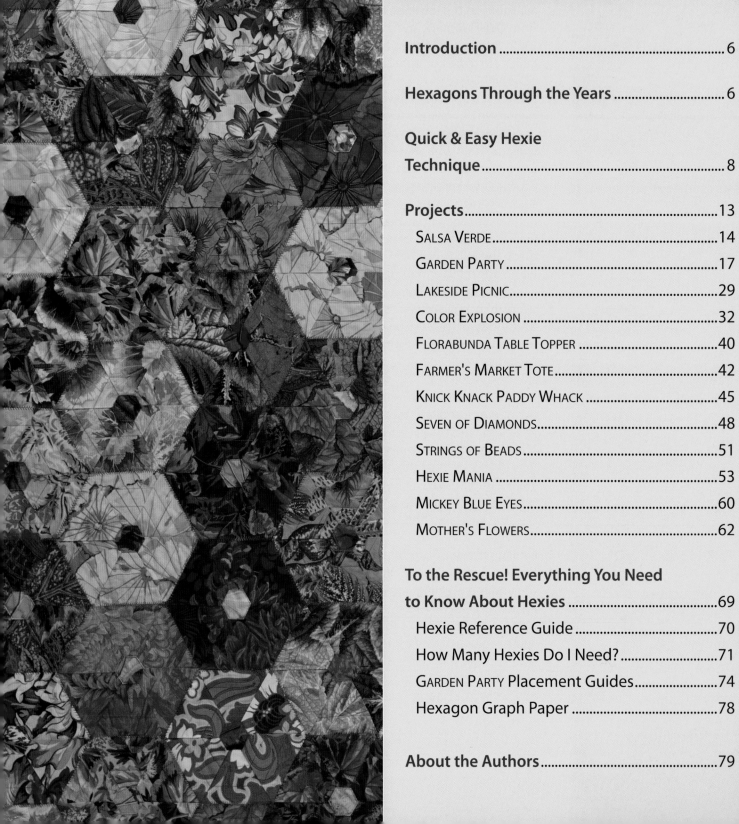

Contents

Introduction

Quick and Easy Hexie Quilts is a technique book, a project book, and a reference guide, providing a different way to make hexies and a variety of projects in which to use them. Gone are English paper piecing and plastic templates! Gone is that dreaded basting step! With a few folds and a few stitches, a circle of fabric becomes the perfect hexie for your next project.

Though still sewn by hand, the Quick and Easy Hexie technique turns out hexies much faster than more traditional methods. This process originated in the Appalachians by women who traced a circle on fabric using a canning jar lid. Why did they use the canning jar lid for a template? Back in those days, every woman had a ready supply of these! When visiting one another, everyone always had the same size template on hand.

These same jar lids are still used as templates today, though, as shown by the many projects in this book, any size circle will work. And, with the advent of affordable fabric die cutters for home use, circles can easily be cut en masse in a variety of sizes.

Be sure to refer to the To the Rescue! section for a go-to source for everything hexie-related:

Handy Hexie Reference Guide lists what size circles you'll need to make various sizes of hexies, along with the associated yardage of fabrics needed.

How Many Hexies Will I Need?—a helpful guide to determine how many hexies will be required for projects.

Hexagon Graph Paper—use colored pencils to design your own hexie masterpiece!

We hope you enjoy our modern take on hexies! Join us for more hexie inspiration at thehexieblog.blogspot.com!

Hexagons
Through the Years

An extensive search on the Internet verifies that the hexagon is one of the oldest patterns in the history of quiltmaking. It is believed to be the first pieced quilt pattern ever published in the United States. It appeared in *Godey's Lady's Book* (Volume 10, pg. 41) in January, 1835. Barbara Brackman dates the earliest known hexagon patterns at 1817 (*Clues in the Calico: A Guide to Identifying and Dating Antique Quilts*, pg. 169). One of the earliest documented hexagon quilts is dated 1800 to 1820 and was shown in *Through the Needle's Eye: The Patchwork and Quilt Collection at York Castle Museum*. In this quilt, the hexagons were pieced together in rows, but in this same publication, several Grandmother's Flower Garden quilts are shown and they date from 1820 to 1900. Pieced hexagon quilts have roots in England and some hexagon templates discovered date back to around 1770 (Illinois State Museum: Keeping Us In Stitches: Quilts and Quilters: Pieced Quilts: Hexagon).

Through the years hexagon quilts have been called Mosaic, One-Patch, Honeycomb, Honeycomb Patchwork, Beehive, Six-Sided Patchwork, Bride's Bouquet, French Bouquet, French Rose Garden, and Flower in the Field, to mention just a few names. The most popular and recognizable hexagon quilt pattern, however, has always been Grandmother's Flower Garden. These quilts contain a center hexagon circled by six colorful printed or solid hexagons with another row of twelve hexagons around that. The increased popularity of the Grandmother's Flower Garden pattern during the 1920s and throughout the 1930s may be attributed to many factors. It was the Great Depression, times were hard financially, and many women quilted out of necessity. Grandmother's Flower Garden could be made with small scraps, some as tiny as 1", and the colorful "flower gardens" served as happy reminders of better times. This provided a much-needed lift to their spirits during these difficult years.

Though the individual hexagons, sometimes called "sixes," can and have been arranged in many different patterns, there are some constants that have remained through the years. Green hexagons are frequently used to separate the flower units and it is said they represent grass or garden pathways. When white hexagons are used to separate the flower units, they are reminiscent of white picket fences. Yellow around the flowers is said to represent the sunshine in the garden. Occasionally, odd-colored hexagons were strategically mixed with the green paths; they became stepping stones.

Even in this age of speed-cutting and piecing, the versatility of hexagons may account for their enduring popularity among quiltmakers. Perhaps hexagons are appealing to quilters because they give the illusion of a circle even though they are individually constructed to form straight edges and offer the ease of sewing straight edges together to create patterns. The hexagon is one of the most versatile of all geometric shapes. It can stand side by side with other hexagons of the same size, or be combined with other sizes and geometric shapes to create designs of amazing complexity.

The construction of hexagons is still first and foremost a process that works best as a hand project. The English paper-piecing method has remained the most commonly used method of making hexagons, but through the years various other techniques have come on the market. Reusable plastic and Mylar® templates, made by Quilt Patis and Brandy's, were introduced several years ago to eliminate the paper templates and make the process quicker and easier.

In December 1979, Quilt World included an article describing how to convert a circle into a hexagon. The article suggested that a "jar lid" be used for the pattern. Unlike the method featured in this book, the folds were made but the stitching was not done until all of the folds were in place. The article suggested "stuffing" the hexagons with cut-up stockings if you did not want to leave them flat. Similar variations appeared on the Internet in 2008 and 2011 and the method was called "Folded Hexagon Yo-Yo" or "Hexagon Yo-Yo." Using this method produced quilts that were reversible since the back side looked as good as the front. Instead of adding batting and backing, these quilts were used in the Deep South as lightweight summer spreads. The question may be asked if these are "real" quilts since they do not have batting and backing and may not be quilted. Is a Cathedral Window a quilt even though it does not have batting and backing and is not quilted? Absolutely, it is a quilt! Consequently, hexagon quilts that begin with the circles of fabric folded into the hexagon shape, whether or not they include batting or quilting, are quilts in the truest sense of the word.

As is evidenced by the increased number of hexagon quilts that are found on the Internet, it is clear the pattern has certainly withstood the test of time, and is destined to remain a favorite among quilters of all ages.

Since making hexagons from circles of fabric, as described in this book, is faster, easier, can go anywhere, and yields workable hexagons of any and all sizes—at least one hexagon quilt, whether traditional or contemporary, may just be in the future of all quilters.

Quick and Easy Hexie Technique

Our Quick and Easy Hexie Technique is different than most. Instead of using hexagon-shaped paper or plastic templates, we start by cutting fabric into a circle. With a few folds and stitches, a circle quickly becomes a hexagon. At the end of the project, there are no pieces of paper or plastic to remove from the hexagons. What a time-saver!

To cut circles from fabric, you can do it the tried-and-true way, if you like. Use a compass to draw a circle template of the correct size. Cut out the template, trace circles onto fabric, and cut them out with scissors. Or simply look around your home; you already own lots of circle templates! How about using a large-mouth canning jar lid? The top to a peanut butter jar? A saucer or plate?

But if you want to cut lots of circles quickly, do as we do: use a die-cutting machine! We use the AccuQuilt® die cutter. AccuQuilt has a variety of circle die sizes, in addition to other fun dies! Some of the available dies are clear, allowing for easy fussy-cutting. You can even have custom dies made as we did for the 14" circles in HEXIE MANIA.

However you choose to cut your circles, we know you'll have fun making hexies the Quick and Easy Hexie way!

MAKING HEXIES

You will need fabric, round template, scissors, pencil, thimble (optional), needles, and thread. We typically use a thread color that matches the fabric. For multicolored fabrics, we use a neutral beige or gray or a monofilament thread in clear or smoke. We prefer quilting betweens needles, size 10.

For optimum accuracy, lightly starch and press fabric before cutting circles.

1. Start by tracing a circle on the back of the fabric. The circle can be any size, as long as the size is consistent for hexies that are to be sewn together (Fig. 1).

2. Cut out the circle along the drawn line (Fig. 2).

3. Thread a needle; doubling the thread. Knot the ends together (Fig. 3).

4. Fold the circle of fabric in half, right sides together (Fig. 4).

5. Fold in half again (Fig. 5).

6. Insert the threaded needle into the center of the fold. Take only a little nip of the fabric—a few threads of fabric is enough (Fig. 6).

7. Pull the needle through the fabric until the knot catches (Fig. 7).

Fig. 1

Fig. 2

Fig. 3

Fig. 4

Fig. 5

Fig. 6

Fig. 7

Fig. 8

Fig. 9

Fig. 10

Fig. 11

Fig. 12

Fig. 13

Fig. 14

Fig. 15

8. With the wrong side of the fabric facing up, insert the needle approximately ⅛" or less from the edge of the fabric circle at one of the fold lines. The needle should go through the fabric from the wrong side (Fig. 8).

9. Pull the thread taut, allowing the edge of the circle to fold to the center of the circle where the knotted end of the thread is located (Fig. 9). Finger-press the fold.

10. Insert the needle on the right end of the folded edge, through both layers of fabric, again approximately ⅛" or less from the fabric edge (Fig. 10).

Note: If you are left-handed, you may find it easier to work around the circle in a counterclockwise motion. Insert the needle on the left end of the folded edge. The end result will be the same.

11. Pull the thread taut so that the edge of the circle folds to the center of the circle. Finger-press (Fig. 11).

12. Moving clockwise around the circle, again insert the needle on the right end of the last fold, ⅛" or less from the edge of the circle (Fig. 12).

13. Pull thread taut. Finger-press (Fig. 13).

14. Continue moving clockwise and insert the needle as before. After this step, the two longest folds should be parallel to each other (Fig. 14).

15. Repeat again. After this step, the fabric should look like this, with a point on one end (Fig. 15).

16. Insert needle into the point, approximately ⅛" or less away from the edge (Fig. 16).

17. Pull the thread taut and you have a hexie! Take a small stitch, running the needle through the stitch to anchor the thread. Snip the thread. We will now call the folded side of the hexagon the back side (Fig. 17).

18. We will call the flat side of the hexagon the right side (Fig. 18). Now wasn't that quick and easy?

Fig. 16

Fig. 17

Fig. 18

SEWING THE HEXIES TOGETHER

1. Hold two hexies right sides together. Using a needle that has been double threaded and knotted, insert the needle through both hexies at one end of the folded edges (Fig. 19).

2. Whipstitch the hexies together, making stitches through the edge of each. You only need to catch a few threads of each hexie with each stitch. End by knotting the thread; then snip (Fig. 20).

3. The hexie units should look like this from the front (Fig. 21).

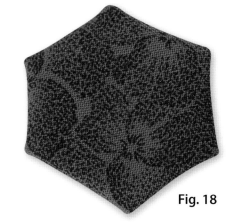
Fig. 19   **Fig. 20**

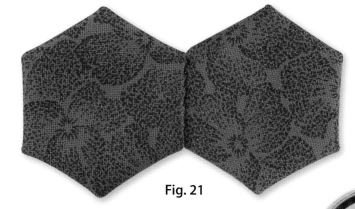
Fig. 21

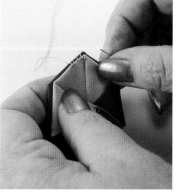

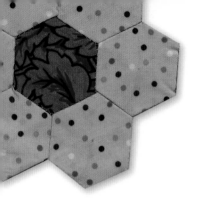

FLOWER UNITS

To make a **single-flower unit**, rows 1 and 3 will each have two hexie petals joined together. Row 2 will have the flower center with a hexie petal on either side (Fig. 22).

To make a **double-flower unit**, rows 1 and 5 will have three hexies stitched together; rows 2 and 4 will each have four hexies stitched together; and the center row will have five hexies stitched together. Once you have all three (or five) of these rows done, simply slip stitch or whipstitch each row together (Fig. 23).

This method reduces the number of starts and stops and allows maximum efficiency and speed to complete the design.

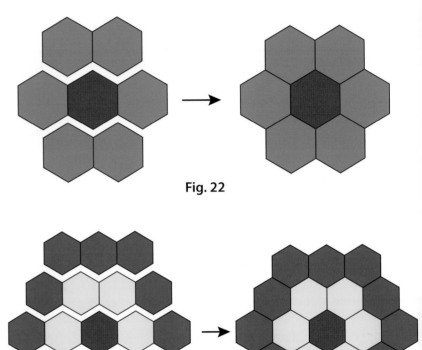

Fig. 22

Fig. 23

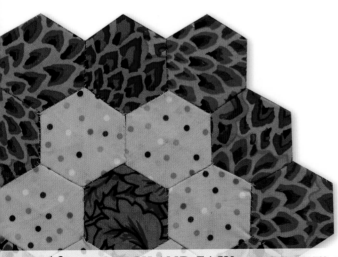

the PROJECTS

SALSA VERDE
Designed and made by Julia C. Wood
Professionally quilted by Elayne Vognild

SALSA VERDE

SALSA VERDE is a fabulous way to use your stash.
Create eye-catching hexie flowers displayed in a modern configuration. Change the background color to suit your taste and needs. No matter what color you choose, this quilt will surely draw attention!

Quilt size 60" x 70"	**Fabric Credit: Kona® Cotton Solid Artichoke**
Skill Level: Beginner	**AccuQuilt® Die: 3" circle**

FABRIC REQUIREMENTS

Background
- 4 yards

Hexagons
- 4 yards of assorted fabrics
  (One fat quarter of fabric (18" x 22") or ¼ yard of fabric (9" x 42") will yield 39 circles 3".)

CUTTING DIRECTIONS

Background fabric
- 1 piece: Width of fabric x 2 yards
- 1 piece: 22" x 72"

Hexagons
Cut 603 assorted 3" circles

INSTRUCTIONS

1. Make 27 double-flower units, each containing one center hexagon, six hexagons for the first round of petals, and 12 hexagons for the second round of petals, as shown in the Technique section.

2. Stitch nine double-flower units together by hand, as shown in Fig. 24. Repeat for the other 18 double-flower units, making three strips of nine flower units.

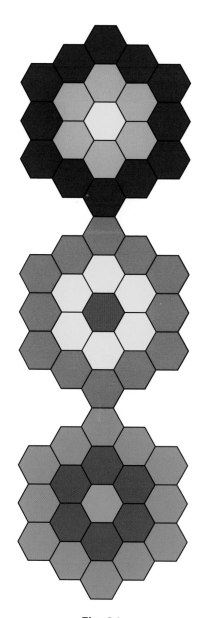

Fig. 24

3. Make hexies from the remaining 90 circles, sewing them together into two lengths of 45 hexies. (Fig. 25)

4. Stitch the two background pieces together along the length of the fabric. Press the seam to one side; press the entire background.

5. Pin one of the strips of single hexies centered along the seam line on the background. The top hexie should be placed 1" from the top of the background. Continue to pin down the length of the seam line, ending 1" from the bottom of the background fabric.

6. Appliqué the row of hexies to the background (by hand or machine).

7. Pin a row of double-hexie flowers so that it is centered 10" to the side of the single-hexie row. Stitch down as before. Continue to pin and stitch alternating rows of single hexies and hexie flowers, keeping each vertical row centered 10" from the next.

8. Quilt and bind as desired.

Fig. 25

Garden Party

Thirties Garden Party
Designed, made, and quilted
by Dr. Peggy G. Rhodes

. . . .

Quilt size 34" x 31"
Skill Level: Beginner to Advanced
AccuQuilt® Dies: 3" and 4" circles

Oriental Garden Party
Designed, made, and quilted
by Dr. Peggy G. Rhodes

. . . .

Quilt size 38" x 35"
Skill Level: Beginner to Advanced
AccuQuilt® Dies: 3" and 4" circles

*GARDEN PARTY **may be one of the easiest
and most fun projects you can make.***
Follow the design or be inspired to create your own
dimensional basket of flowers. By varying the size of the hexies,
joining them in different configurations, using both the front
and back of the hexies, and adding a few buttons or beads, you
will have the perfect arrangement for your next garden party.

FABRIC REQUIREMENTS

Background, Backing, and Sleeve

2½ yards of muslin or 1 yard of prequilted fabric
with ½ yard of a matching solid fabric (brown or
color of your choice)

Basket

1 fat quarter (basket-weave fabric or fabric of your
choice)

Flower Petals

THIRTIES GARDEN PARTY	ORIENTAL GARDEN PARTY
5 fat quarters	7 fat quarters
(or ¼ yard pieces)	(or ¼ yard pieces)
Dark pink	Red
Light pink	Orange
Lavender	Turquoise
Blue	Light mauve
Peach	Dark mauve
	Blue
	Purple

Flower Centers

3 yellow (Thirties) or 5 gold (Oriental) fat quarters
(or scraps)

Stems and Leaves

½ yard green (enough to make all the stems, but
you may prefer to get fat quarters of 3 to 5 different
greens to have a variety of stems and leaves)

Batting

(If you are quilting your background) 1 square
yard of Hobbs Heirloom® 80/20 Blend (or use your
favorite batting)

Binding

Use scraps from the flowers and leaves or some of
the extra ½ yard of fabric purchased to match the
background/backing/sleeve.

OTHER SUPPLIES

THIRTIES GARDEN PARTY
White buttons: (1 baby button; 19 shirt buttons;
1 medium button)

ORIENTAL GARDEN PARTY
8mm beads (to match Flower 3)

Circle Templates

4" circle (if not using the AccuQuilt® Dies)
Wide-mouth canning lid (approximately 3¼" circle)
3" circle (if not using the AccuQuilt® Dies)
Regular canning lid (approximately 2⅝" circle)

*Note: darker flowers and leaves will need smoke
instead of clear invisible thread*

.004 clear invisible nylon thread (Sew Art
International is my favorite.)

Clover® #12 Bias Tape Maker—½"
Clover #18 Bias Tape Maker—¾" (ORIENTAL GARDEN PARTY)
Blue disappearing pen (or a pink air disappearing pen)
Quilting bar/edge guide for your machine, if quilting
own background
Open-toe foot for sewing machine
505® Spray Adhesive
Strips of ¼" Lite Steam-A-Seam 2® (or other double-
sided fusible web)
Spray starch (optional)
Iron and pressing surface

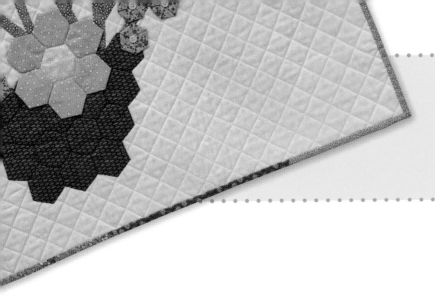

Optional - before cutting, starch the fabric for the flowers, leaves, and stems. This takes time and effort but the results are worth it. You will have less raveling, the folds will be clean and crisp, the strips will be straighter, and the appliqué will have little to no puckering.

THIRTIES CUTTING DIRECTIONS

Background and Backing
Cut 2 pieces of muslin that measure 36" x 32" (or simply add 1" to both the width and height measurements of the finished wallhanging.)

Sleeve
Cut 1 strip 6½" from the remaining muslin. This will make a 3" wide sleeve. If you prefer a 4" sleeve, cut an 8½" strip.)

Dark pink
1. Cut 4 circles 4"
2. Cut 1 regular lid circle

Light pink
1. Cut 13 wide-mouth lid circles

Lavender
1. Cut 9 circles 3"
2. Cut 11 regular lid circles

Blue
1. Cut 8 circles 4"
2. Cut 8 circles 3"

Peach
1. Cut 8 circles 4"
2. Cut 4 circles 3"

Yellow #1 (for blue flowers)
1. Cut 2 circles 4"
2. Cut 2 circles 3"

Yellow #2 (for light pink flowers)
1. Cut 2 wide-mouth lid circles
2. Cut 1 regular lid circle

Yellow #3 (for peach flowers)
1. Cut 2 circles 4"

Stems and Leaves
(can all be from same fabric or multiple greens – as long as stems and leaves match for each flower.)
1. Fold the ½ yard diagonally on the bias and cut 5 bias strips 1" wide for stems
2. Cut 5 circles 4"
3. Cut 8 circles 3"

If you have additional green fabric, you may want to cut more circles for leaves. Also, you may prefer "real" looking leaves instead of the hexie leaves.

Binding
Cut 2" strips from the leftover fabric from the flowers and leaves. These strips can be straight of grain. You will need approximately 142" of binding.

Basket
Cut 18 circles 4"

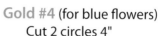

ORIENTAL CUTTING DIRECTIONS

Background
Cut the prequilted fabric to 36" x 39" (or, simply add an inch to both the width and height measurements of the finished wallhanging.)

Sleeve
Cut one strip 6½" from the solid fabric that matches the prequilted background. This will make a 3" wide sleeve. If you prefer a 4" sleeve, cut an 8½" strip.

Red
Cut 15 circles 3"

Orange
1. Cut 6 circles 4"
2. Cut 6 wide-mouth lid circles
3. Cut 3 regular lid circles

Turquoise
1. Cut 8 circles 3"
2. Cut 13 regular lid circles

Light mauve
1. Cut 8 wide-mouth lid circles
2. Cut 1 circle 3"

Dark mauve
Cut 12 wide-mouth lid circles

Blue
Cut 8 circles 4"

Purple
1. Cut 6 circles 4"
2. Cut 3 regular lid circles

Gold #1 (for red flowers)
Cut 3 circles 3"

Gold #2 (for orange flowers)
1. Cut 1 wide-mouth lid circle
2. Cut 1 circle 4"

Gold #3 (for light and dark mauve flowers)
1. Cut 4 wide-mouth lid circles
2. Cut 1 circle 2"

Gold #4 (for blue flowers)
Cut 2 circles 4"

Gold #5 (for purple flowers)
Cut 1 circle 4"

Stems and Leaves
(Can all be from same fabric or multiple greens – as long as stems and leaves match for each flower.)

Green #1
1. Cut 2 bias strips 1¼" wide
2. Cut 2 bias strips 1" wide
3. Cut 4 circles 4"
4. Cut 6 wide-mouth jar lid circles

Green #2
1. Cut 1 bias strip 1¼" wide
2. Cut 3 bias strips 1" wide
3. Cut 2 circles 4"
4. Cut 8 wide-mouth jar lid circles
5. Cut 2 circles 3"

Green #3
1. Cut 1 bias strip 1¼" wide
2. Cut 3 bias strips 1" wide
3. Cut 4 wide-mouth lid circles
4. Cut 1 small lid circle

Green #4
1. Cut 1 bias strip 1" wide
2. Cut 1 regular lid circle

If you have additional green fabric, you may want to cut more circles for leaves. Also, you may prefer "real" looking leaves to the hexie leaves.

Binding
Cut 5 strips 2" wide from the leftover solid fabric that matches the background.

Note: Cut these strips the size that you prefer to use in binding. I use 2" straight of grain. You will need approximately 170" for the binding.

Basket
Cut 18 circles 4"

INSTRUCTIONS

Background

One of the best things about GARDEN PARTY is that the background is crosshatch-quilted before the appliqué is done or you can use prequilted fabric and skip the quilting.

1. If you are quilting the background and want to use the exact placement of stems shown in the samples, enlarge the line drawings provided on pages 74–77 to trace the stems onto your background fabric or use the diagram below to mark your stem placement (Figs. 26a–26b).

   Be careful to note that the beginnings of the stem "branches" are placed under the main stem. Since the drawn lines will be covered up, it is okay to use a pencil to trace them. Follow the directions on the sheet for proper placement. If you prefer to create your own arrangement, there is no need to mark before quilting.

Quilting the background

2. Using a ruler with a 45-degree angle and a blue disappearing pen, draw one line for vertical stitching and another for horizontal. These lines should be close to the center of your background and will form an "x." You will probably need a longer ruler to extend the lines from top to bottom and from side to side (Fig. 27).

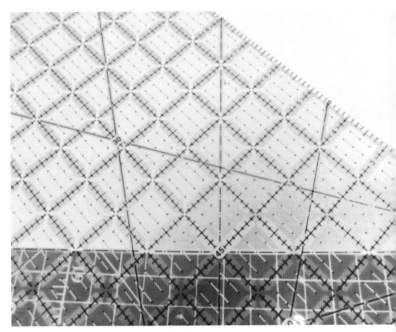

Fig. 27

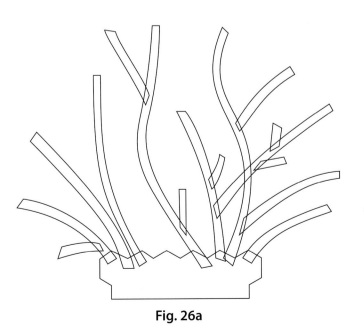

Fig. 26a

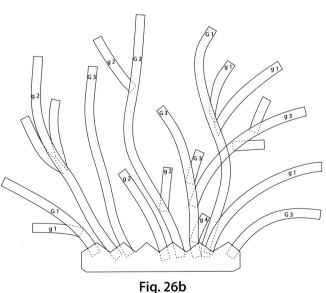

Fig. 26b

3. Layer the backing, batting, and background into a quilt sandwich. Use 505 Spray to secure the layers together or, if you prefer, use your favorite basting method of holding the sandwich together.

4. Attach the seam guide to your machine exactly 1" to the right of the needle. Stitch on top of each of the drawn lines with thread that matches the background. (When these lines are quilted, remove the markings.)

5. Use the seam guide to stitch exactly 1" away from each of these lines. Each new line of stitching creates the "guide" line for the next stitching line. It helps to keep the quilt "in square" if you alternate your stitching between the two directions. Continue this process until the entire background is crosshatch quilted (Fig. 28).

MAKING AND ASSEMBLING THE HEXIES AND STEMS FOR THIRTIES GARDEN PARTY

1. Use the ½" bias tape maker to make 1" strips into bias stems. Use the ¾" bias tape maker to make 1¼" strips into bias stems. If you do not have a bias tape maker, fold the sides of the strips toward the middle and press.

2. Cut the ¼" Steam-A-Seam 2 to the length of each stem. Iron the adhesive side to the back of each stem. Remove the paper. This allows you to position the stems in place on the background without pins. You will appliqué the stems later so this adhesive replaces the need for pins and secures them in place until the stitching is complete. It is not a permanent adhesive (Fig. 29).

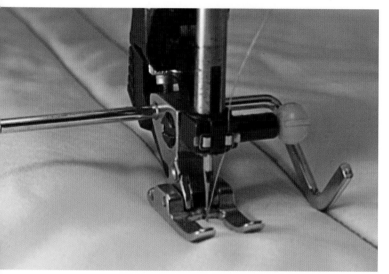

Fig. 28

Fig. 29

3. From the yellow #1 circles, take two of the 3" circles and from yellow #3, take one of the 3" circles. Fold each of these circles in half and then in quarters and tack. These will be used for the bud "inserts."

4. Use all of the remaining circles to make hexies by following the instructions in the Technique Section.

5. Match a large yellow #1 center hexie with six of the large blue hexies and another large yellow #3 center hexie to six of the large peach hexies. Follow the instructions in the Technique Section to whip-stitch the hexies into flowers.

6. Match a 3" yellow #1 hexie with six blue hexies 3" and whipstitch into a flower.

7. Select two wide-mouth jar lid size yellow #2 hexies to go with 12 of the light pink hexies. Join the hexies to make two flowers.

8. Whipstitch two of the large 4" blue hexies together; then whipstitch the unit onto a large 4" green hexie. Pin one of the yellow #1 bud inserts in place (Fig. 30).

9. Whipstitch two of the 3" blue hexies together; then whipstitch the unit onto a green 3" hexie. Using the last yellow #1, pin in place the 3" bud insert.

10. Whipstitch two of the 4" peach hexies together; then whipstitch the unit onto a 4" green hexie. Pin in place the remaining yellow #3 bud insert.

11. Whipstitch two of the 3" peach hexies together; then whipstitch one of the 3" peach hexies to one of the green 3" hexies. Whipstitch these two units together with the green hexie in the middle of the three peach hexies (Fig. 31).

12. Whipstitch two of the 4" dark pink hexies together. On the center of one side of this unit, whipstitch another of the large dark pink hexies. In the center on the other side of the hexie unit, whipstitch a 4" green hexie (Fig. 32).

13. Take the remaining peach 3" hexie and, with the back-side up, place it on top of a large 4" green hexie (centered with straight edges matching). Sew the medium button in the center to anchor the hexies together (Fig. 33).

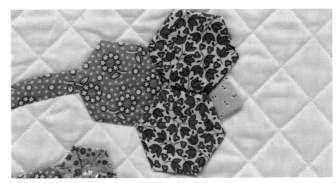

Fig. 30

Fig. 31

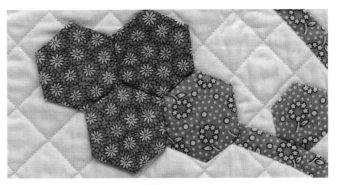

Fig. 32

Fig. 33

14. Similar to the bud in step 13, place the small jar lid dark pink hexie on top of the remaining 4" dark pink hexie and secure with a tiny baby white button.

15. Layer the remaining 4" green hexie, the wide-mouth lid light pink hexie, and the small jar lid yellow hexie. Using monofilament thread, appliqué around the top yellow hexie. This will hold all three hexies in place. If you prefer, this unit can also be secured with a button instead of appliquéing the yellow center (Fig. 34).

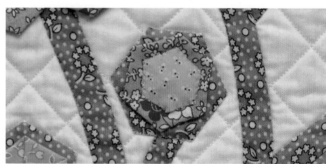

Fig. 34

16. Whipstitch a row of three basket hexies; a row of four basket hexies; a row of five basket hexies; and a row of six basket hexies. Whipstitch the rows together to form a graduated basket with the row of three hexies on the bottom and the row of six hexies on the top.

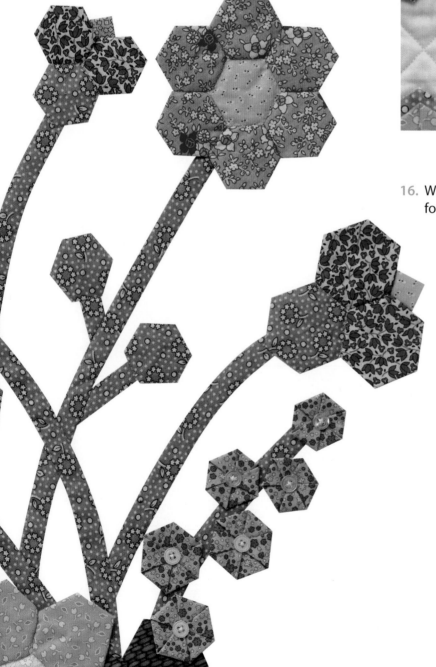

ARRANGING AND COMPLETING
THIRTIES GARDEN PARTY

1. Machine set-up: Use a very fine bobbin thread that matches the background (60 weight/2-ply or 80 weight/2-ply fine machine embroidery thread works great). Pre-wound bobbins usually have very fine thread and provide a good option. Thread the machine with .004 Invisible Nylon Thread (I prefer Sew Art International brand). Use a sharp 60/8 or 65/9 needle.

2. Set your machine to the blind hem stitch (three to seven straight stitches on the right and then a zigzag to the left). Set the stitch width to very narrow—just wide enough for the zigzag to catch two to three threads of the appliqué fabric. The distance between the zigzags should only be about ⅛" or less. Anything more will produce gaps along the edge of the appliqué. Practice with a sample to get the length and tension adjusted correctly before starting on GARDEN PARTY.

3. If your machine does not have a blind stitch, use a very narrow blanket stitch or a narrow zigzag stitch but neither will look as much like mock hand appliqué. Use an open-toe foot so that you can see the stitches. The straight stitches should be just off the edge of the appliqué fabric and the zigzag will only slightly catch the appliqué fabric. Be sure you do not have the single needle plate on your machine.

4. If you quilted your own background, you already have your stem placement marked. Observe that the beginnings of the "branches" are placed under the main stems. If the stems cross, it doesn't matter which one is ironed in place first.

5. If you are using a prequilted background, trace the diagram onto tissue paper and center it over your background. Pin one side of the tissue to the edge of the background so that it can easily be raised to place your stems on the background. Lay out the stems being careful to place the beginnings of the stem "off-shoots" under the main stems.

6. Once in place, iron the stems down and begin appliquéing. If you are creating your own design, play with the stem placement until you are pleased. Remember to leave enough room at the bottom of the background for the basket.

7. Place the bottom of the basket 2¾" from the bottom of the quilted background. Center the basket and pin in place. Appliqué the basket to the background, leaving the top of the basket open. The stems will appear to go into the top of the basket.

8. Look at the picture and place the large blue and large peach hexie flowers in their designated spots. Appliqué around the center hexies; then in the seams that join each of the petals together. Leave the outer edges loose for a three-dimensional effect.

9. Put the three smaller flowers—two pink and one blue—in place and appliqué.

10. Put the two-hexie bud units in place. Appliqué around the green hexies and along the bottom left and bottom right sides of the blue and pink hexies. Appliqué down the middle seam of each set—this will secure the yellow buds pinned in place. By hand (or machine), tack down the flower points on either side of the yellow bud inserts.

11. Put the three-hexie petal units in place—dark pink and peach. Appliqué around the green hexies and along the seams between each of the hexie petals.

12. Pin the lavender hexies in place (folded-side up) along the two "empty" stems. The stem on the left needs six of the 3" hexies and seven of the small lid hexies. The remaining lavender hexies should be placed on the stem on the right. Begin with one of the smaller hexies at the top of each of the stems and alternate the hexies around the stems. Place the smaller hexies near the upper parts of the stems and the larger hexies around the lower halves of the stems. Secure the hexie petals in place with white shirt buttons. The edges of these hexies are not appliquéd—they are held in place by the buttons.

13. Pin the layered hexie petals in place—dark pink, light pink, and peach. Appliqué around the bottom hexie.

14. Put the hexie leaves in place and appliqué around each one. If you choose to use "real" shaped leaves, you may wish to anchor them with stitched veins rather than appliqué.

15. Square the wallhanging and add a sleeve, if desired.

16. If you used the muslin background and wish to use the multi-fabric binding, sew the binding strips together (straight seam) using at least one of each of the colors. The strip lengths should range from 6" to 18". The longer strips should be used to turn the corners to avoid having an extra seam allowance in the miter. You will need approximately 142" for the binding.

17. Bind the quilt, apply your label, and your THIRTIES GARDEN PARTY is finished!

MAKING AND ASSEMBLING THE HEXIES AND STEMS FOR THE ORIENTAL GARDEN PARTY

1. Use the ½" bias tape maker to make 1" strips into bias stems. Use the ¾" bias tape maker to make 1¼" strips into bias stems. If you do not have a bias tape maker, fold the sides of the strips toward the middle and press.

2. Cut the ¼" Steam-A-Seam 2 to the length of each stem and iron the adhesive side to the back. Remove the paper. This allows you to position the stems in place on the background without pins. You will appliqué the stems later so this adhesive replaces the need for pins and secures them until the stitching is complete. It is not a permanent adhesive.

3. Follow the instructions in the Technique Section, make hexies from all of the circles of fabric.

4. Make two red flowers using six hexies each with gold #1 centers.

5. Whipstitch three red hexies to a gold #1 center, as shown. Pin the bud's gold center on top of a 4" green #1 hexie. It will be appliquéd in place later (Fig 35).

Fig. 35

6. Make one large and one small orange flower with gold #2 centers.

7. Make one light mauve flower with a gold #3 center.

8. Whipstitch the two remaining light mauve hexies together. Whipstitch this unit to a green #2 hexie of the same size and pin the remaining small gold #3 hexie between the light mauve unit to form a bud (Fig. 36).

Fig. 36

9. Use six dark mauve hexies and one gold #3 hexie to make a flower.

10. Use three of the dark mauve hexies and one green #2 same size hexie to make a bud (Fig. 37).

Fig. 37

11. Using two dark mauve hexies and one green #2 hexie same size, make a bud as described in step #8. Pin the gold #3 hexie in place at the top.

12. For the final mauve single-hexie bud, begin with one large green #2 hexie (right-side up) and stack the remaining dark mauve hexie (folded-side up) on top of it. Add the small light mauve hexie (folded-side up) and top with the small gold #3 hexie (right-side up). Secure the stack by tacking the 6 points of the small gold hexie (Fig. 38).

Fig. 38

13. Make a blue flower—six hexie petals with a gold #4 center.

14. Use the two remaining blue hexies and the remaining gold #4 hexie to construct a bud like the one in step 8 in the Thirties assembly section.

15. Make a purple flower—six hexie petals with a gold #5 center.

16. With the remaining three purple hexies and a green #4 hexie, make a bud like the one in step 10.

ARRANGING AND COMPLETING YOUR
ORIENTAL GARDEN PARTY

1. Machine set-up: Use a very fine bobbin thread that matches the background (60 weight/2-ply or 80 weight/2-ply fine machine embroidery thread works great). Pre-wound bobbins usually have very fine thread and provide a good option. Thread the machine with .004 Invisible Nylon Thread (I prefer Sew Art International brand). Use a sharp 60/8 or 65/9 needle.

2. Set your machine to the blind hem stitch (three to seven straight stitches on the right and then a zigzag to the left). Set the stitch width to very narrow—just wide enough for the zigzag to catch two or three threads of the appliqué fabric. The distance between the zigzags should be about ⅛" or less. Anything more will produce gaps along the edge of the appliqué. Practice with a sample to get the length and tension adjusted correctly before starting on your GARDEN PARTY.

3. You can use a very narrow blanket stitch or a narrow zigzag stitch but neither of these will look as much like mock hand appliqué. Use an open-toe foot so that you can see the stitches. The straight stitches should be just off the edge of the appliqué fabric and the zigzag will only slightly catch the appliqué fabric. Be sure you do not have the single needle plate on your machine.

4. If you quilted your own background, you already have your stem placement marked. Observe that the beginnings of the "branches" are placed under the main stems. If the stems cross, it doesn't matter which one is ironed in place first.

5. If you are using the prequilted background, trace the diagram onto tissue paper and center it over your background. Pin one side of it to the edge of the background so that it can easily be raised to place your stems on the background.

6. Lay out your stems being careful to place the beginnings of the stem "off-shoots" under the main stems. The capital "G" denotes the wider stems and

the lower case "g" represents the thinner stems. The numbers refer to the different green fabrics.

7. If you have chosen to create your own design, play with the stem placement until you are pleased. Remember to leave enough room at the bottom of the background for the basket.

8. Once in place, iron the stems down and appliqué.

9. Place the bottom of the basket 2¾" to 3" from the bottom of the quilted background. Center the basket and pin in place. Be sure the bottoms of the stems are covered by the top of the basket. Starting and ending at the first point on the top row, appliqué the basket to the background leaving the top of the basket open.

10. Refer to the large picture on page 17 to determine placement and pin all of the buds in their appropriate places. Be careful to cover at least ½" of the stem tops. Appliqué the outside edges of the bud units' green and gold hexies to the background. Stitch in the ditch the seams on the inside of the bud units. Backstitch several stitches to lock the thread in place. Tack, by hand or machine, the points of the flower petals to the background. This will give a three-dimensional effect.

11. Pin the flowers in place. Flowers and buds of the same color are placed on the same colored stems. Stitch in the ditch around each flower center and in the seams between the petals. Backstitch several stitches to lock the thread in place. Tack the points of each flower petal to the background.

12. If you are using the hexie leaves, you may wish

to join a smaller hexie to a larger hexie to make a longer leaf. The sample has a double leaf of this type from green #1 and green #2. Another option is to join two of the smaller green hexies together for a different longer leaf (green #3).

13. If you are using "real" shaped leaves, you may wish to anchor them with stitched veins rather than appliquéing around each one.

14. Refer to the large picture to determine the placement of the leaves. Note that you can attach the point, as well as the straight side of a hexie, to the stem. The leaf may also be placed on the side of the stem as well as angled on top of the stem. When you are satisfied with your placement, pin in place, and appliqué around each leaf.

15. Place the turquoise hexies (folded-side up) along the two "empty" stems. The stem on the left will have five large hexies and nine smaller ones. The stem on the right will have three large hexies and four smaller ones. Begin with one of the smaller hexies at the top of each of the stems and alternate the hexies around the stems. The smaller hexies are around the upper parts of the stems and the larger hexies are placed around the lower halves of the stems. Secure these hexie petals in place with beads. The edges of these hexies are not appliquéd —they are held in place by the beads.

16. Square the wallhanging, add the sleeve (if desired) and bind with the fabric that matches your background. Apply the label and your Oriental Garden Party is finished!

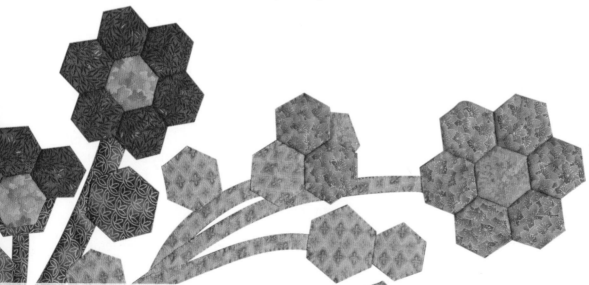

LAKESIDE PICNIC
Designed and made by Julia C. Wood
Professionally quilted by Elayne Vognild

Allow yourself to dream...

about a sunny afternoon picnic with icy glasses of lemonade as you make happy hexie flowers for this fun quilt. Since the flowers are made from multiple fabrics, you can make the most of your stash and use those scraps. The flowers are appliquéd onto a crisp white on white background. One of the borders features hexies that are reminiscent of a flowering-vine swag.

Quilt size 70" x 78½"
Skill Level: Intermediate

Fabric Credit: (Hexies) DS Quilt Collection for Fabric Traditions
AccuQuilt® Die: 4" circle

FABRIC REQUIREMENTS

Background (white)
1½ yards + 2 yards for Border 1

Hexies
Flowers: 2¾ yards of assorted fabrics

Borders
Border 1: 2¾ yards of assorted fabrics
Sashing and Border 2 (red dot): 2 yards
Border 3 (blue stripe): 2 yards

CUTTING DIRECTIONS:

Flower background squares
Cut 30 squares 8"

Single-flower units
Cut 7 circles 4" for each of 30 flowers (6 of one fabric and 1 from another fabric for the center of flower) for a total of 210 circles.

Sashing
1. Cut 24 strips 1½" x 7½"
2. Cut 7 strips 1½" x 39"
3. Cut 2 strips 1½" x 49½"

Background for Border #1
1. Cut 2 strips 10" x 49½"
2. Cut 2 strips 10" x 60"

Hexies for Border #1
Cut 220 circles 4"

Border #2
Cut 2 strips 1½" x 62" and 2 strips 1½" x 68½"

Border #3
Cut 2 strips 4½" x 70" and 2 strips 4½" x 70½"

MAKING THE QUILT CENTER

1. Make 210 hexies for the single-flower units. Make 30 single-flower units, as illustrated in the Techniques Section.

2. Appliqué (by machine or hand) each single-flower unit to an 8" flower background square, making sure to align all flowers the same way (Fig. 39).

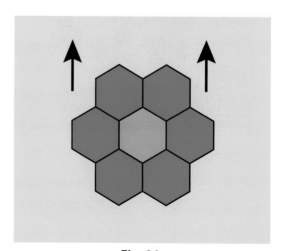

Fig. 39

3. Trim squares to 7½".

4. Sew a 1½" x 7½" sashing strip to the right side of 24 squares, pressing seams toward sashing strips.

5. Sew four sashed squares together and one plain square on the right to make a row of five squares. Repeat for the remaining squares, making six rows. Press seams towards sashing.

6. Sew a 39" sashing strip to the bottom of each of the six rows. Press seams toward the sashing strips.

7. Sew rows together. Press seams toward the sashing strips.

8. Sew the remaining 39" sashing strip to the top of the set of rows, pressing toward the sashing strip.

9. Sew the two 49½" sashing strips to the sides of the set of rows, pressing seams toward the sashing strips.

Border #1

1. Sew the 10" x 49½" border #1 strips to the sides of the quilt. Press seams toward the border. Sew the 10" x 60" border #1 strips to the top and bottom of the quilt.

2. Make hexies for border #1 from the 220 circles.

3. Arrange hexies on border #1 as shown in the quilt photograph. Pin in place and appliqué (by hand or machine) to the border.

Note: You may choose to hand stitch these hexies together before pinning and appliquéing them in place.

Border #2

1. Sew the 68½" border #2 strips to the sides of the quilt, pressing seams away from center of quilt.

2. Sew the 62" border #2 strips to the top and bottom of the quilt, pressing seams away from center of quilt.

Border #3

1. Sew the 70½" border #3 strips to the sides of the quilt, pressing seams away from center of quilt.

2. Sew the 70" border #3 strips to the top and bottom of the quilt, pressing seams away from center of quilt.

Quilt as desired.

COLOR EXPLOSION

Designed and made by Dr. Peggy G. Rhodes

Professionally Quilted by Elayne Vognild

Quilt size 45½" x 33½"
Skill Level: Advanced (or confident intermediate)
AccuQuilt® Die: 4" circle

Create your very own impressionistic watercolor masterpiece by using hexagons.

Though the use of hexagons is more difficult than most watercolor processes, the technique is still the same. Color saturation and depth is created through the strategic placement of colors according to light, medium, and dark values. Start with your own stash of colorful scraps and yardage and you may be able to design your work of art without purchasing anything new. Approximately 100 different fabrics were used to make the hexies for COLOR EXPLOSION.

FABRIC SELECTION

For watercolor, it is generally preferred to use multicolored prints such as:

- Florals (realistic or stylized)
- Paisleys (curled teardrops in many sizes)
- Decorative geometrics (avoid straight lines and sharp, jagged points)
- Theme prints (fruits, vegetables, birds, fish, scenics, tropicals, holidays, etc.)

The fabric should not "read" as a solid; it should have some type of texture to it. The lighter "lights" have a light design on a light background and the darker "darks" have a dark design on a dark background. The effect you are going for is to have your eye move continually from one hexagon to the next. A solid color or a straight or jagged line will cause your eye to pause and break up the continuity of the whole. This process can also be accomplished with gradated solids; though very pretty, the solids do not provide the same impressionistic feeling.

If you are still unsure as to fabric selection, look through several "Color Splash" or "Watercolor" books before proceeding.

FABRIC REQUIREMENTS

It is very difficult to calculate the exact yardage needed to make a watercolor project. Since you are shading the colors from light to dark, it is not an exact science. With some fabrics you may be able to achieve the move from light to dark with three hexies and with others it may take a dozen or more. This project was designed to use the colorful florals and prints in your stash. If you find your stash lacking in any of the colors you want to use, purchase the desired fabric in fat quarters or in ⅛ yard pieces. You want to use as many different fabrics as possible in the watercolor. You may use only one hexie from some fabrics and several from others.

Binding

- ½ yard or pieced strips to match the edges of the design. Approximately 170" are needed.

Other Supplies

- Spray starch (optional but very helpful)
- Monofilament thread (clear and smoke) or thread to match the fabrics
- Fabric paint or dye pens (optional)
- Reducing glass/camera/copier/Ruby Beholder® Value Finder (any of these will help you really "see" the design)

FABRIC PREPARATION

Before cutting, heavily starch the fabric. You will easily get clean, crisp folds and the raveling will be greatly reduced.

CUTTING DIRECTIONS

1. Cut 4" circles from the scraps and yardage. You will probably need 800 or more before you complete the project.

   If the fabric has a large amount of blank space between patterns, you will need to fussy cut the circles from the designs.

2. Binding: If you want to use one fabric for the binding, cut five 2" strips the width of the fabric.

3. Join the strips with a diagonal seam. If you prefer a wider binding, you may need more fabric. If you want the binding to match the edges of the finished quilt, you can piece leftover fabric to match the edges, and then cut the 2" binding strips.

INSTRUCTIONS

1. Make hexies from all of the 4" circles.

Remember – your fabric has two sides and you've paid for both of them. Check the back of the circle, and if it looks a little lighter, make some hexies with the back of the fabric showing, as well as some with the front side showing.

Here are several examples of using both the front and back sides of the fabric (Fig. 40):

Fig. 40

2. Sort the hexies by color (Fig. 41).

Fig. 41

3. Working with one color at a time, divide the hexies into a minimum of three stacks—light, medium, and dark values (not necessarily colors). If you can't determine the value, place the hexies on your copier and print a black and white (not color) copy. You will quickly see the differences among the values of the fabrics of each color. Do this step for each of your colors (Fig. 42).

Fig. 42

Fig. 43

Fig. 44

Fig. 45

4. If you do not have really light values in your different colors, go back to your stash and see if you can find background fabric that has just a little color to it such as swirls, smudges, etc., but no straight lines, or checks (Fig. 43).

5. Once you have sorted each of the colors, determine which color groupings you want to include in your quilt. Nothing says you have to use them all. I did not have much contrast in the greens so I chose to leave them out of COLOR EXPLOSION.

6. Working with one color at a time, arrange the hexies into a pattern. It is much easier to lay out the design on a table top rather than a design wall because you will move the hexies many times before you are pleased. Always begin with the darkest darks, add the medium darks, move to the lightest darks, the darkest mediums, mediums, lightest mediums, darkest lights, medium lights, and end with the lightest lights.

You have several options regarding the arrangement of each color grouping. Use all or any combination to create interest within your watercolor. Do not think about the size of your wallhanging at this point; concentrate on developing color saturation by using the values from darkest dark to lightest light. When the colors are developed, you can then push them closer together and blend the lighter and/or darker colors to establish the size of the wallhanging.

For the corner placement, choose the strongest color grouping you have and place as many as 15 or so of the darkest dark hexies in a corner of the wallhanging. Using the progression of values from darkest to lightest of this color, place more hexies in a semicircle around these dark ones. This strong color will set the boundaries for the sides of that particular corner of the wallhanging. You may use this same corner placement design for one or more of the other colors; it is your choice (Fig. 44).

For the edge placement (Fig. 45), select another color grouping and begin by placing several of the darkest-dark hexies in a straight line (can be vertical or horizontal). From here you will build the darkest to lightest hexies from only one side (left, right, top, or bottom).

For the inside or center, place the darkest hexies in the middle and then work out until the lightest are all the way around the dark center. It will look as though the color exploded on all sides (Fig. 46).

Note: Some colors naturally tend to blend from one to another. When this happens you may not need to go all the way to the lightest lights before moving into a new color (e.g., deep purple blends into dark maroon and dark maroon can easily move into deep burgundy and burgundy blends into dark red, etc.)

Fig. 46

7. Continue this process for each color grouping. Remember that you do not have to, and probably will not, use all the hexies that you have for any of the color groupings. Your goal is to blend each color from one to the other. Use the design (e.g., leaves, curved lines, petals, etc.) and color to gradually move from dark to light. Rotate the hexies to determine the best placement for each one. Ideally, your eye will move right across the edges of the hexies without even realizing where one starts and another one stops (Figs. 47–48).

Note: You can use fabric dye or paint pens to darken and/or blend areas that need just a little boost. It is best to do this after the hexies are sewn together. Be careful not to overuse the pens because you will lose texture (the dye or paint goes on very flat).

Fig. 47

8. By now you can tell whether or not you need to purchase additional fabric with specific colors and values to complete the impressionistic design. Though batiks are not usually the best fabric for watercolor quilting (they tend to read solid), the lightest lights will frequently have just enough texture and color to allow you to easily use them to move from one color grouping to another. A reducing glass or a camera lens can help you spot problem areas in the total design because you can see the whole design at once.

9. Begin to slide all of the color groupings together, adding new hexies where needed. This is a tedious process and you may need to step away from it for brief intervals or even several hours. Frequently, when returning rested, you are able to immediately see what needs to be moved or added to make the colors "fit together." Allow several days or weeks to complete this step. The creative process cannot be rushed. If you've completed other watercolor

Fig. 48

projects using squares, you will notice how much harder it is to work with hexagons; the result is well worth the effort. This is definitely a "hands-on" process. You may spend hours getting a 5" square section just perfect and that is absolutely fine.

10. Will you ever be completely satisfied with your design? Probably not. At some point, however, you will be satisfied enough with what you see and you will then be ready to sew the hexies together.

11. Sew each vertical row together using a whipstitch as described on page 11 in the "Sewing the Hexies Together" technique section. To avoid confusion later, label each row 1, row 2, etc. Use a safety pin or a straight pin to attach the hexies in order in each row.

12. To avoid having to change thread colors, use either a clear or smoke monofilament thread to stitch the hexies together. Double knot and/or backstitch both the beginning and end of each of the joining seams. The last thing you want is for the stitches to come loose.

Fig. 49

13. After the rows are together, join row 1 to row 2. Add row 3. I preferred to add one or two rows at a time because it is easier to hold the addition in my hand. If you have help, each of you can start on opposite ends sewing the rows together; then join the two halves. It is not necessary to pin the rows in place but it is essential that the point of each hexie is in the center of the matching seam in the row to which it is being sewn. The row numbers should stay attached until finished (Fig. 49).

14. If the sides of two hexies being joined are not exactly the same length, you can easily make them fit together. Match the beginning and end points and curve the shorter side of the hexie around your thumb to sew the hexies together. The two sides will magically match as you join the seam (Fig. 50).

15. When the rows are sewn together, use the fabric paint or dye pens to eliminate any bold lines or color mismatches that were created at the seams where the hexies join together.

16. The sample does not include a border, but you can add one. Either appliqué the zigzag edges

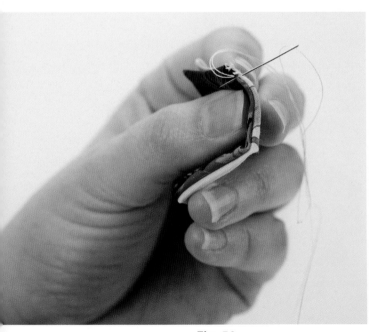

Fig. 50

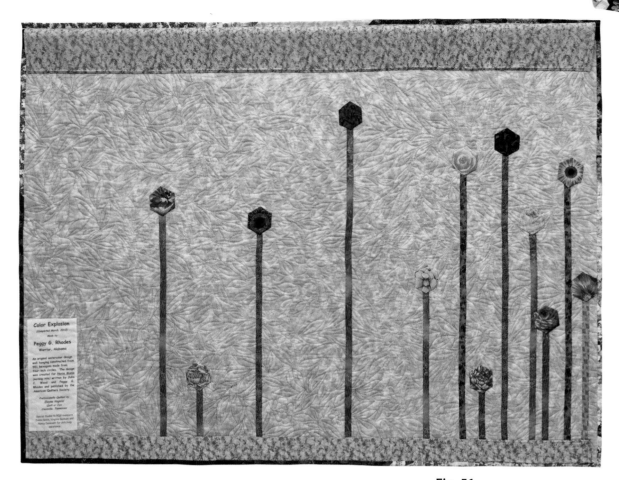

Color Explosion
(Completed March 2012)
Made by
Peggy G. Rhodes
Warrior, Alabama

An original watercolor design
wall hanging constructed from
951 hexagons made from
four-inch circles. The design
was created for Hexie Quilts
(working title) written by Julia
C. Wood and Peggy G.
Rhodes and published by the
American Quilters Society.

Professionally Quilted by
Elayne Kingrea
Quilt as You
Greenville, Tennessee

Special thanks to AQS members
Dawn Seals, Virginia Baskett and
Nancy Donovan for stitching
assistance.

Fig. 51

onto the border or "square" the quilt by cutting off the zigzags. Be sure to do a row of stay-stitching before cutting the hexies.

17. Quilt as desired. The hexies are double thickness and quite dense. Use a somewhat heavier backing or starch it to avoid tucks and wrinkles while quilting. No matter how careful the quilter, it is possible to have some tucks on the back. When this happens, get creative. You may end up liking the back of the quilt as much as you do the front (Fig. 51).

18. If you are not adding a border, it is better to quilt before cutting off the zigzag edges. Once the top is quilted, square it up.

19. Add a sleeve, label, and bind either with a single piece of fabric or pieced strip that is made to "match" the edge colors of the wallhanging (Fig. 52).

Congratulations! You have just created your own impressionistic masterpiece.

Fig. 52

FLORABUNDA TABLE TOPPER

FLORABUNDA TABLE TOPPER
Designed and made by Julia C. Wood

A simple and fast project, this round table topper has no batting.

Grab your stash of scraps, cut some circles, and you'll be done in no time! A felt backing finishes the back. What a wonderful gift this will be!

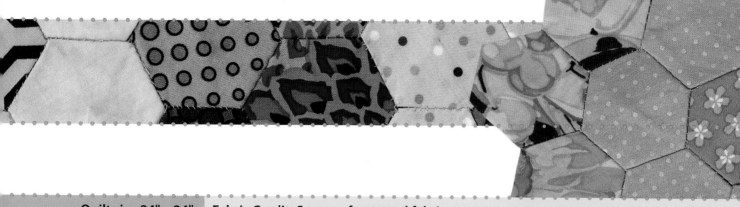

Quilt size 24" x 24"
Skill Level: Beginner

Fabric Credit: Scraps of assorted fabrics
AccuQuilt® Die: 4" circle

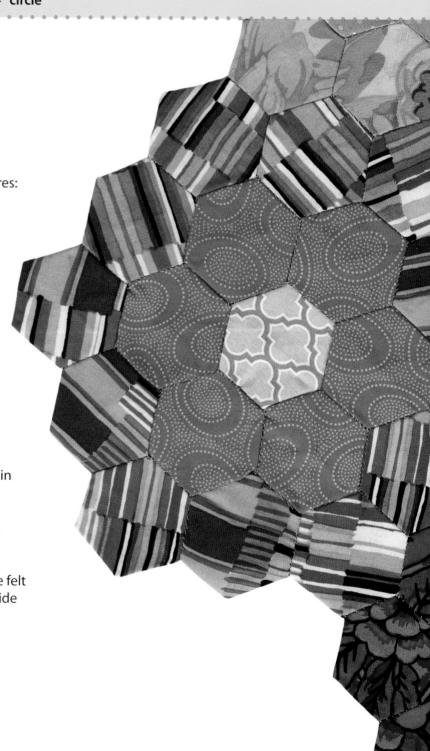

FABRIC REQUIREMENTS

Total fabric required: 3 yards of scraps
Each of the seven double-petal flower units requires:
   1 circle 4" of fabric A
   6 circles 4" of fabric B
   12 circles 4" of fabric C

CUTTING DIRECTIONS

Cut scraps into 4" circles.

Backing
   25" square of felt

INSTRUCTIONS

1. Make seven double-flower units as illustrated in the Technique section.

2. Sew the double-petal flower units together as indicated in photo.

3. Trim felt to fit the table topper. Hand stitch the felt to the back of the table topper along the outside edge.

FARMER'S MARKET TOTE
Designed and made by Julia C. Wood

A durable bag with large hexies spanning the sides and bottom…

this tote will become your new favorite for shopping, travel, or to take along your current sewing project. A handy drawstring allows for easy closure. *Let's get to the market!*

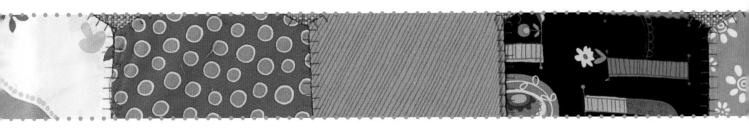

Tote size 17" x 17" x 5"	Fabric Credit: Hexies: Wee Woodland by Keiki for Moda
Skill Level: Intermediate to Advanced	Lining: Kona Cotton
	AccuQuilt® Die: 8.5" circle

FABRIC REQUIREMENTS

Bag fabric
1 yard home décor fabric (60" wide)

Lining fabric
1½ yards

Hexie fabric
¾ yard (or a 9" square of 11 different fabrics)

Drawstring fabric
⅛ yard

Other supplies
Four wooden beads, 1" with large holes

Drawstring
Cut one piece 2" x 40"

Drawstring casing
Cut one piece 44" x 2⅝"

Hexies
Cut 11 circles 8½"

CUTTING DIRECTIONS

Bag fabric
Front/Back: Cut two from enlarged bag template
Sides/Bottom: Cut one piece 6" x 53"
Handle: Cut one piece 5" x 34"

Lining fabric
Front/Back: Cut two from enlarged bag template
Sides/Bottom: Cut one piece 6" x 53"

Center Top

Enlarge 450%
(Actual size 18" x 18")

Cut 2 from outer fabric.
Cut 2 from lining fabric.

Center Bottom

FARMER'S MARKET TOTE **Template**

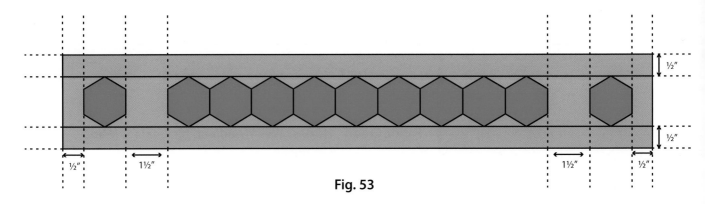

Fig. 53

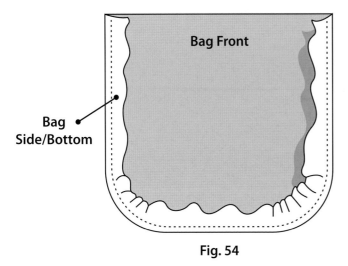

Bag Front

Bag
Side/Bottom

Fig. 54

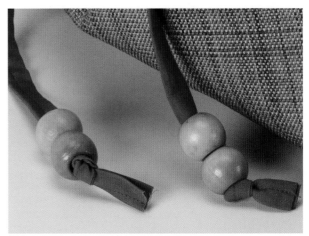

Fig. 55

INSTRUCTIONS

1. Make 11 hexies per Technique section.

2. Pin hexies to the Side/Bottom piece of the bag fabric (Fig. 53).

3. Sew hexies in place using a machine blanket stitch.

4. Pin and sew one bag front to side/bottom piece using a ½" seam allowance. Repeat for other side of bag (Fig. 54).

5. Pin and sew one bag front lining to side/bottom lining. Repeat for other side of bag lining.

6. Fold and press ½" under on each long side of the bag handle. Press the handle in half lengthwise. Stitch ¼" from either side.

7. Press under ½" of the upper edge of both the bag and the bag lining.

8. Pin bag handles to inside of purse sides, placing each end of handle 1½" below top edge of bag. Pin

lining to bag around top edges, making sure the bag and lining edges are even. Stitch together bag and lining at the top edge: seam allowance should be ⅛". Reinforce handle by stitching the ends of the bag a second time.

9. Fold and press under ½" along short sides of drawstring casing. Fold and press under ¼" along long sides of drawstring casing.

10. Pin casing to exterior of purse, leaving 2" gap in center of one side. Stitch ⅛" from top and bottom of casing. Note: Stitch the casing through both the bag exterior and the lining.

11. Fold and press under ½" of the long sides of drawstring. Fold and press in half with the raw edges on the inside. Stitch down the length of the drawstring.

12. Run drawstring through casing opening using a safety pin or bodkin. Slide two beads on each end of drawstring, tying knots to secure (Fig. 55).

KNICK KNACK PADDY WHACK

Designed, made, and quilted
by Julia C. Wood

Quilt size: 52" x 82"
Skill Level: Beginner
AccuQuilt® Dies: 8.5" circle
Fabric Credit: Assorted Scraps

KNICK KNACK PADDY WHACK *is a whimsical zigzag quilt sure to be loved by all.* Each zigzag row can be made with the same fabric, or you can use various fabrics of the same color family.

FABRIC REQUIREMENTS

A. Ten zigzag rows require 25 circles 8½" (1¾ yards of fabric) each for a total of 17½ yards
B. One partial zigzag row requires 15 circles 8½" (1 yard of fabric)
C. One partial zigzag row requires 16 circles 8½" (1 yard of fabric)
D. One partial zigzag row requires three circles 8½" (¼ yard of fabric)
E. One partial zigzag row requires four circles 8½" (¼ yard of fabric)

CUTTING DIRECTIONS

Cut fabric into circles as indicated above.

INSTRUCTIONS

1. Make a hexie from each circle according to the Technique Section.

2. Using the set of 15 "B" hexies and the set of three "D" hexies, sew three triangular units (Fig. 56).

3. Whipstitch one set of 25 "A" hexies into a zigzag row as shown (Fig. 57).

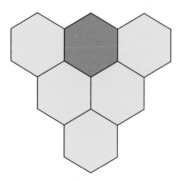

Fig. 56

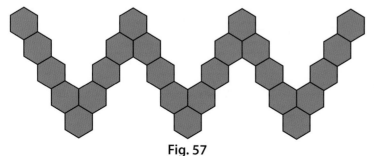

Fig. 57

4. Whipstitch the three triangular units to the zigzag row. This will be the top of the quilt (Fig. 58).

5. Continue to make "A" hexies into zigzag rows and stitch them to the previous zigzag row on the quilt.

6. Using the set of 16 "C" hexies and the set of four "E" hexies, sew units as illustrated (Fig. 59).

7. Whipstitch these units to the last (bottom) zigzag row as illustrated (Fig. 60).

8. Quilt as desired.

FINISHING

Trim batting even with outer edges of hexies. Trim the backing fabric ¾" from edge of hexies and cut a slit at each inner corner. Fold backing in over batting, tucking under quilt top. Hand stitch edges closed (Fig 61).

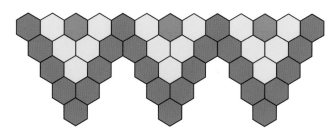

Fig. 58

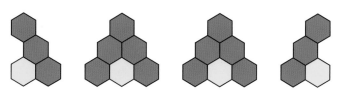

Fig. 59

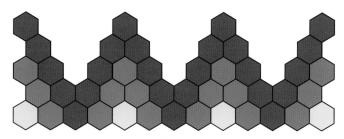

Fig. 60

Fig. 61

SEVEN OF DIAMONDS

Designed and made by Julia C. Wood

Professionally quilted by Elayne Vognild

Quilt size 44" x 62"

Skill Level: Intermediate

AccuQuilt® Die: 3.5" circle

With its playful combination of fussy-cut and strip-pieced hexies…

the traditional diamond pattern is transformed into a contemporary baby quilt or a comforting lap quilt.

Note: Fussy-cut means to center a motif in the circle before cutting.

SEVEN OF DIAMONDS

Finished size 44" x 62" **Skill Level: Intermediate** **AccuQuilt® Die: 3.5" circle**	**Fabric Credit:** **Background: Alexander Henry "Heath"** **Border: Amy Butler's Soul Blossoms for Rowan Westminster Fibers** **Hexies: Various colors of Kona® Cotton Solids by Robert Kaufman and fussy-cut flowers from various colors and prints from Amy Butler's Soul Blossoms for Rowan Westminster Fibers**

FABRIC REQUIREMENTS

Background 1⅔ yards
Border 2 yards
Hexies Solid fabric—14 strips 2½" x 40"
    Floral fabric—7 fabrics, ¼ yard each

Note: If fussy-cutting, additional fabric will be required.

CUTTING DIRECTIONS:

Background One piece 33½" x 52½"
Border Two pieces 33½" x 6½" (top and bottom)
    Two pieces 62½" x 6½" (sides)
Hexies Solid fabrics—see step 2
    Floral fabrics—from each fabric, cut 16 circles 3½", fussy-cutting to center an image in circle as desired.

INSTRUCTIONS

1. Sew two solid strips (with good contrast) together along the long side. Press seam toward darker fabric.

2. Cut eight 3½" circles from each strip-set, making sure the seam line runs through the center of the circle (Fig. 62).

Fig. 62

3. From the step 2 set of eight circles, make six hexies by taking the first stitch at the center edge of one of the strips (Fig. 63).

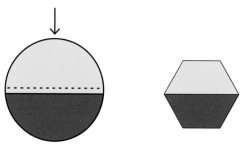

Fig. 63

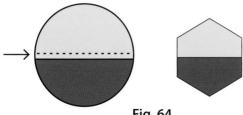

Fig. 64

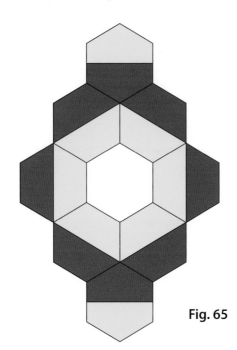

Fig. 65

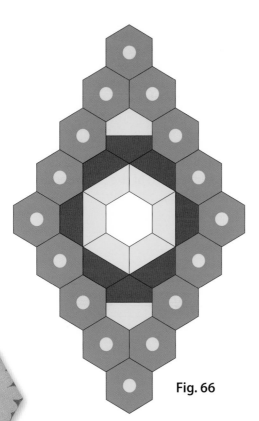

Fig. 66

4. Make two hexies by taking the first stitch at the seam line (Fig. 64).

5. Whipstitch each set of strip-pieced hexies together as shown (Fig. 65), with the hexies made in step 4 at the top and bottom. (Note: There will be no hexie in the center.)

6. Make hexies from the 16 fussy-cut floral circles. Whipstitch to the perimeter of the hexie unit made in step 4 (Fig. 66).

7. Pin and appliqué (by hand or machine) each of the seven hexies units made in step 5 to the background (Fig. 67).

8. Add borders:
   Sew 33½" border pieces to the top and bottom of the quilt top, pressing toward the border.
   Sew 62½" border piece to each side of the quilt, pressing toward the border.

9. Quilt as desired.

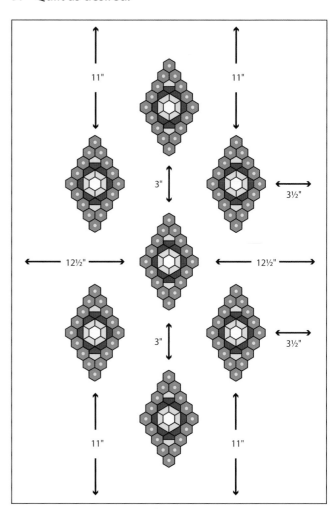

Fig. 67

Strings of Beads

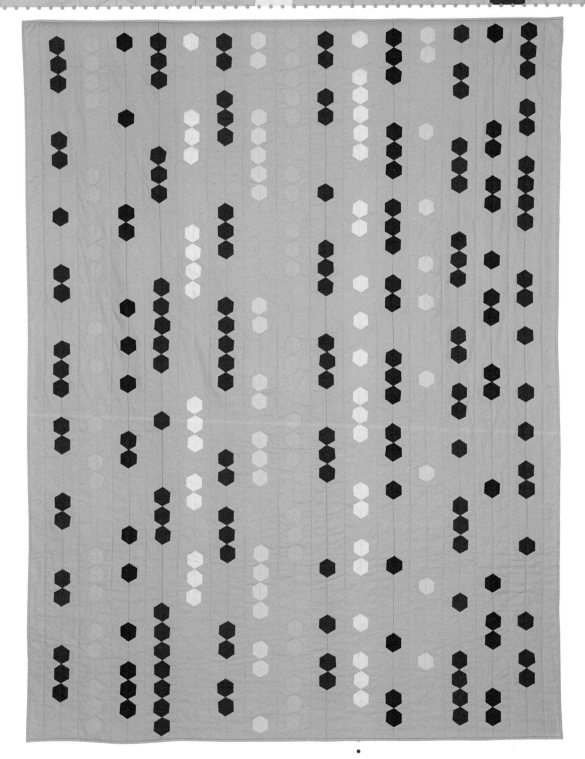

STRINGS OF BEADS

Designed, made, and quilted by Julia C. Wood

Finished size 56" x 73"

Skill Level: Beginner

AccuQuilt® Die: 3.5" circle

STRINGS OF BEADS *is a quick, modern project that produces dramatic results.*
Single hexies made from the same fabric are appliquéd point to point onto a neutral background in a seemingly random pattern. Six different colored "strings of beads" alternate across the quilt. Choose your own favorite color combination and make this design your own!

Fabric Credit: Kona Cotton Solids by Robert Kaufman Fabrics
AccuQuilt® Die: 3.5"

FABRIC REQUIREMENTS

Background 4⅔ yards (color: Kona 1007 Ash)

Hexies ¾ yard each of 6 different colors (Kona 1066 Cerise, 1080 Coal, 142 Crocus, 1234 Mint, 1291 Pink, and 354 Zucchini)

Backing 4½ yards

INSTRUCTIONS

1. Cut background fabric as follows:
   1 piece 40" x 80"
   1 piece 28" x 80"

2. Sew background pieces together along long sides.

3. Cut 60 circles 3½" from each of the six hexie fabrics.

4. Make hexies from the cut circles according to directions in the Technique section.

5. Pin hexies of one color along the vertical seam line on the pieced background; hexies should be placed point to point at random along the seam line, leaving spaces as desired. Each vertical row of hexies should have from 15 to 26 hexies. Appliqué in place by hand or machine.

6. Using a temporary fabric marker or sliver of soap, mark a vertical line 3½" on one side of the center of the sewn hexies.

7. Pin hexies of another color along the marked line at random as before. Appliqué in place.

8. Continue to mark lines 3½" apart, pin hexies along the line, and appliqué in place until there are 15 vertical rows of hexies.

9. Quilt as desired. This quilt is wonderful with vertical straight line quilting, making for a quick finish!

HEXIE MANIA

HEXIE MANIA

Designed, made, and quilted by Dr. Peggy G. Rhodes

Quilt size 90" x 91"

Skill Level: Beginner to Advanced

AccuQuilt® Dies: 14" (custom) & 3" circle

Fabric Credit: Most of these hexies were made using collections from Kaffe Fassett for Westminster & Rowan Fabrics and Phillip Jacobs for Westminster & Rowan Fabrics

Looking for a way to use all those scraps or extra yardage in your stash?

HEXIE MANIA, a scrappy summer spread, provides just that opportunity. Once you make the hexagons from 14" circles, everything else is done on the machine. There is no batting, backing, cost of professional quilting, or binding required. When you complete this project, it is totally reversible since smaller hexies are used to cover the unfinished edges of the large hexagons. It takes a lot of fabric to make this quilt but what quilter doesn't have at least 34 yards of scraps or unused fabric in their stash. If not, what better reason could you have to purchase more fabric than to make this fun, easy quilt!

FABRIC REQUIREMENTS

68 coordinating fabric/scraps of ½ yard each or 34 yards, plus 1 fat quarter.

Each ½ yard yields 3 circles 14"; each yard yields 6 circles 14". The total amount of fabric you need depends on how many hexies you want of any one fabric.

SUPPLIES

Spray starch (optional but helpful)
Open-toe foot for your machine
Lace-edge joining foot or stitch-in-the-ditch foot (Foot has a center "tooth-like" guide that helps to join two pieces of fabric and a wide needle hole to accommodate decorative stitches)
Quilting bar/edge guide for your machine
Coordinating or matching thread (I used Signature Size 40 Color M11 Variegated)

FABRIC PREPARATION

If you think the colors in your fabric may bleed/fade, it is a good idea to pre-wash. Before cutting, heavily starch all of the fabric. You will easily get clean, crisp folds and the raveling will be greatly reduced.

CUTTING DIRECTIONS

1. Cut 203 circles 14". If you do not have access to a die-cutting machine, draw a 14" circle template. Remember, this template will be used hundreds of times.

   Fold a ½ yard cut of fabric in half matching the selvages. Cut two circles as close to the raw edges and selvages of the fabric as possible (the fabric is folded and you are cutting two circles at once). If you are using a one yard cut of fabric, fold as directed, and then fold again to match the raw edges. You will have four layers of fabric and will cut four circles at once. (Fig. 68)

Fig. 68

Open the fabric and cut the third 14" circle from the center of the remaining fabric. If you are using the one yard cut, completely open the fabric, and then fold the center to allow you to cut two more circles (Fig. 69).

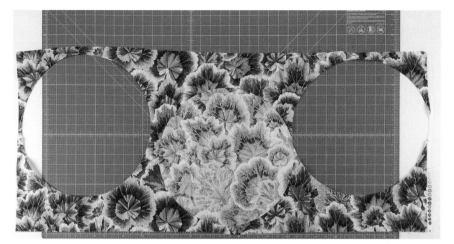

Fig. 69

2. Cut 203 circles 3" from the leftover fabric after cutting the larger circles. (I cut more than what was actually used so that I could mix up the inner hexagons. If you are going to match the inner hexie with the larger hexagon, you will cut the exact number of small circles as you've cut the larger ones.)

3. Optional binding: Since all sides of the quilt are "finished," it is not necessary to add binding. However, if you like the look of a binding and want to add greater stability, you may choose to bind the top and bottom of the quilt. These are straight edges and can easily be bound. From the leftover fabric, cut 2" strips (or the width of binding that you like to use). You will need approximately 226", joined with diagonal seams, to bind the top and bottom. There is no need to use bias binding unless you want to. It is both unnecessary and impractical to bind the zigzagged sides of this quilt.

INSTRUCTIONS

1. Using the instructions in the Technique section, make the 14" and 3" hexagons.

   Since you will be joining the sides of the larger hexies together, it is helpful to pay attention to the measurements of the sides as you make the hexie. Each side of the hexie made from the 14" circle should measure 4". Do not worry if the measurement is a little off; it can be taken up as you join the edges together.

   Note: This is a great "Take-Along" project to work on anywhere. To avoid unnecessary creases in the starched and ironed large circles, use a 15" piece of a foam swimming "noodle" to transport the circles. Wrap the circles around the noodle and secure them with a straight pin stuck right into the noodle.

2. Attach the seam guide to your machine approximately ⅞" from the needle. Place the guide on the edge of the larger hexagon, and using a straight stitch and leaving the needle down, sew from one fold to the next. When you get to the fold, lift the presser foot, and rotate the hexie to sew the straight line to the next fold. This row of stitches should be about ⅞" from the edge but sometimes the placement of the seam guide may vary a little as you rotate the hexie at the fold. It doesn't matter—this project is very forgiving. Just be sure that the stitching from the last fold meets the stitching from the first fold—even if you have to fudge a little and make the last quilted line a little skewed (Fig. 70).

You may prefer to use a decorative stitch instead of the straight stitch for the quilting or to free-motion quilt each hexagon. I used the straight stitch because it was the quickest. The important thing is that all the quilting is done before the hexies are assembled into rows. Remember that the center of each will have one of the smaller hexies added later.

Use variegated thread that has all or most of the colors from the hexies for the quilting unless you prefer to use a solid color. Remember that the quilt will be reversible so be sure to use the same thread in the bobbin.

3. Select 16 of the large hexies to start and end each of the odd-numbered vertical rows. These hexies will not have a smaller center hexie appliquéd on them. Set the seam guide to 1" and stitch an inner row of quilting, using the second row of quilting as your guide.

4. Decide if you want each center hexie to match the larger hexie or if you want to randomly mismatch them as I did. Place a small hexie over the center of the larger hexie where all the folds meet and the thread is knotted. Match the corners of the small hexie with the fold lines of the larger hexie. Match these as closely as you can by rotating the smaller hexie, but it doesn't show if they do not match perfectly. Using a straight stitch as close to the edge as possible, sew the small hexie in place. Overlap several stitches to "lock" in place (Fig. 71).

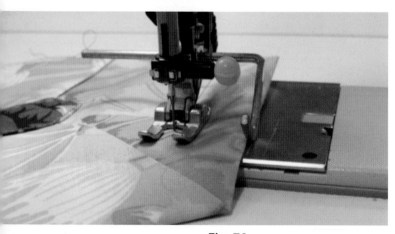

Fig. 70

Fig. 71

5. Once all the hexies have been quilted, lay them out on the bed, or place them on a large design wall to determine the final arrangement. Use the side of the hexagons with the folds as the quilt front. Start and end all of the odd numbered vertical rows with one of the hexies that does not have a smaller center hexie. The hexies can be rotated any way as long as a straight edge is at the top and bottom of each vertical row. HEXIE MANIA has 14 hexies in the first vertical row and 13 in the second vertical row. There are 15 vertical rows of hexagons. Notice that the "zigzag" is formed on each side of the quilt (Fig. 72).

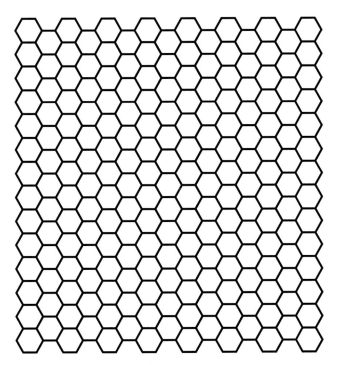

Fig. 72

When the quilt is finished you can decide which side you like best for the front. I preferred to use the side that shows the folds as the front.

6. Fold in half and pin the hexagons that do not have smaller center hexies. These are the ones at the top and bottom of all odd-numbered vertical rows. The folds and unfinished center will be to the inside and the widest part of the hexagon will now form the top (or bottom) of the half hexie (Fig. 73).

Fig. 73

7. Pin or stack each of the vertical rows together and label each row across the top (e.g., 1-1, 2-1, etc.).

8. Make sure the needle plate on the machine will accommodate decorative stitching. Attach the lace-edge joining foot or stitch-in-the-ditch foot. You don't have to use this foot but the small "tooth" in the center of it makes it easier to feed the two hexies together more evenly (Fig. 74).

Fig. 74

Fig. 75

Fig. 76

Fig. 77

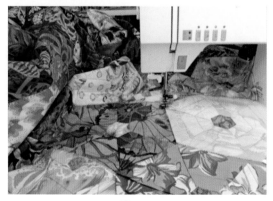

Fig. 78

9. Experiment with several decorative stitches to determine which one you would like to use to join the hexies together. I used the feather stitch (also called the fagoting stitch). Be sure to fold several pieces of fabric together and test the stitch.

10. Beginning with vertical row 1, you are going to sew hexie 1-1 to hexie 1-2. At the beginning and end, backstitch to lock the stitches. If you don't like the look of the backstitching, tack the ends in place either by hand or machine before you add the decorative stitching. Now add hexie 1-3 to what you've already done. Notice that you will always have only one hexie to the right of the needle (Fig. 75).

11. Even though you tried to make every hexie with a 4" side, occasionally there will be a slight difference in this measurement. Simply match the hexies at the beginning of the seam, then hold the ends together, and allow the machine to evenly feed both hexies. The slight difference will disappear (Figs. 76–77).

12. After you have sewn each of the vertical rows together, you will sew row 1 to row 2. ***Make sure the needle remains in the "down" position as you sew the rows together.*** Yes, this is a zigzag path, but you are going to sew them together with multiple short straight lines. Using the same decorative stitch, sew row1-1 to row 2-1. When you get to the point, lift the presser foot and slightly rotate the two rows so that the next short seam will be straight. At the next point, lift the presser foot leaving the needle down, and rotate the two rows back in the other direction so that the short seam will be straight. It is possible to connect the rows without pinning, but if it will make you feel more secure, pin the short seams together. Double pins work best for this. Instead of pins, I used thin strips of Scotch® Tape which worked great but had to be removed with tweezers.

Continue sewing the rows together (Fig. 78).

13. Once the quilt is completely together, decide if you want to bind the top and bottom edges. If you do not, use the decorative stitch to go around all the edges. For the outer edges, change back to the open-toe foot rather than the lace-edge joining foot or stitch-in-the-ditch foot (Figs. 79–80).

Fig. 79

Fig. 80

14. If you've decided to bind the top and the bottom, do not add the decorative stitching to these edges. Cut two binding strips that are 1" wider than the top and bottom edges of the quilt. Fold the binding in half horizontally and sew to the top of the quilt leaving ½" on either side. Press the binding away from the front of the quilt. Working from the back of the quilt, fold the extra ½" toward the back on each side and pin. Pull the binding strip to the back and hand stitch in place (Fig. 81).

Fig. 81

MICKEY BLUE EYES

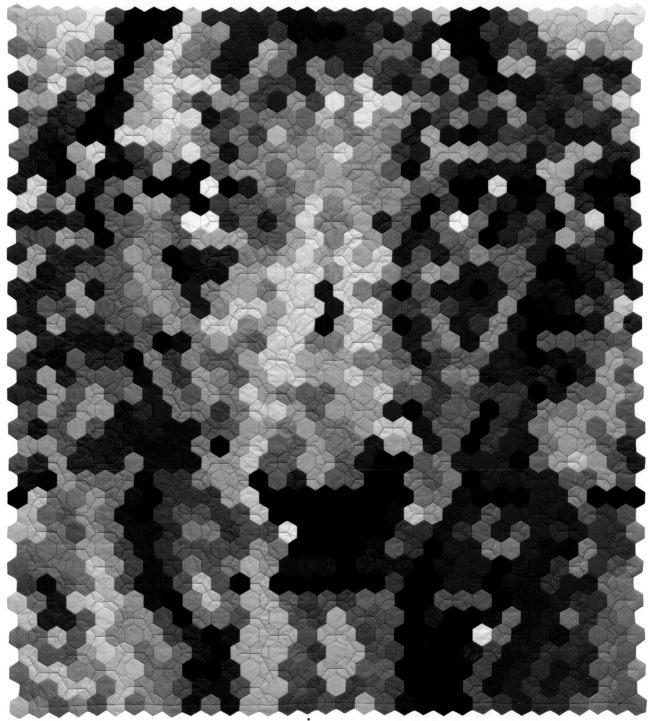

MICKEY BLUE EYES
Designed, made, and quilted by Julia C. Wood

MICKEY BLUE EYES depicts one of Julia's dachshunds, a blue-eyed dapple.
Always enamored with portrait quilts, Julia found a way to make one from hexies! To make the pattern, a photograph was pixelated with software and duplicated in hexies.

SEVEN OF DIAMONDS

Designed and made by Julia C. Wood
Professionally quilted by Elayne Vognild

Quilt size 44" x 62"
Skill Level: Intermediate
AccuQuilt® Die: 3.5" circle

With its playful combination of fussy-cut and strip-pieced hexies...

the traditional diamond pattern is transformed into a contemporary baby quilt or a comforting lap quilt.

Note: Fussy-cut means to center a motif in the circle before cutting.

4. Whipstitch the three triangular units to the zigzag row. This will be the top of the quilt (Fig. 58).

5. Continue to make "A" hexies into zigzag rows and stitch them to the previous zigzag row on the quilt.

6. Using the set of 16 "C" hexies and the set of four "E" hexies, sew units as illustrated (Fig. 59).

7. Whipstitch these units to the last (bottom) zigzag row as illustrated (Fig. 60).

8. Quilt as desired.

FINISHING

Trim batting even with outer edges of hexies. Trim the backing fabric ¾" from edge of hexies and cut a slit at each inner corner. Fold backing in over batting, tucking under quilt top. Hand stitch edges closed (Fig 61).

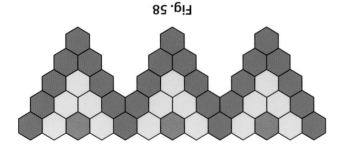

Fig. 58

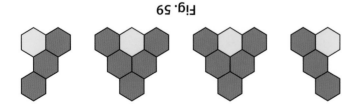

Fig. 59

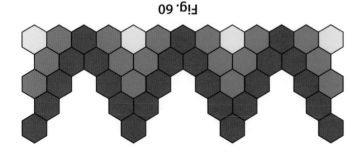

Fig. 60

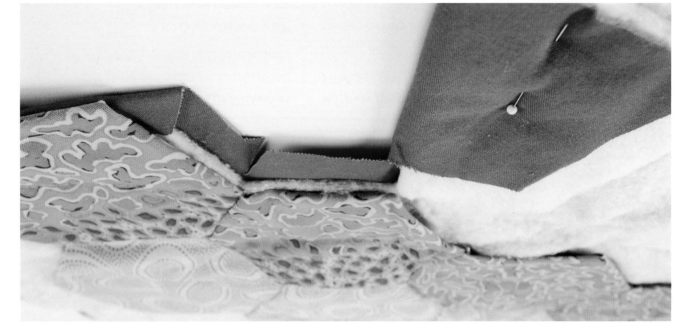

Fig. 61

LAKESIDE PICNIC
Designed and made by Julia C. Wood
Professionally quilted by Elayne Vognild

Allow yourself to dream...

about a sunny afternoon picnic with icy glasses of lemonade as you make happy hexie flowers for this fun quilt. Since the flowers are made from multiple fabrics, you can make the most of your stash and use those scraps. The flowers are appliquéd onto a crisp white on white background. One of the borders features hexies that are reminiscent of a flowering-vine swag.

Quilt size 70" x 78½"
Skill Level: Intermediate

Fabric Credit: (Hexies) DS Quilt Collection for Fabric Traditions
AccuQuilt® Die: 4" circle

FABRIC REQUIREMENTS

Background (white)
1½ yards + 2 yards for Border 1

Hexies
Flowers: 2¾ yards of assorted fabrics

Borders
Border 1: 2¾ yards of assorted fabrics
Sashing and Border 2 (red dot): 2 yards
Border 3 (blue stripe): 2 yards

CUTTING DIRECTIONS:

Flower background squares
Cut 30 squares 8"

Single-flower units
Cut 7 circles 4" for each of 30 flowers (6 of one fabric and 1 from another fabric for the center of flower) for a total of 210 circles.

Sashing
1. Cut 24 strips 1½" x 7½"
2. Cut 7 strips 1½" x 39"
3. Cut 2 strips 1½" x 49½"

Background for Border #1
1. Cut 2 strips 10" x 49½"
2. Cut 2 strips 10" x 60"

Hexies for Border #1
Cut 220 circles 4"

Border #2
Cut 2 strips 1½" x 62" and 2 strips 1½" x 68½"

Border #3
Cut 2 strips 4½" x 70" and 2 strips 4½" x 70½"

MAKING THE QUILT CENTER

1. Make 210 hexies for the single-flower units. Make 30 single-flower units, as illustrated in the Techniques Section.

2. Appliqué (by machine or hand) each single-flower unit to an 8" flower background square, making sure to align all flowers the same way (Fig. 39).

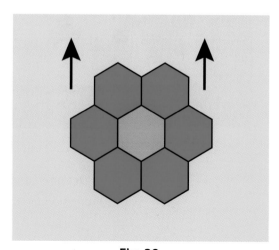

Fig. 39

3. Trim squares to 7½".

4. Sew a 1½" x 7½" sashing strip to the right side of 24 squares, pressing seams toward sashing strips.

5. Sew four sashed squares together and one plain square on the right to make a row of five squares. Repeat for the remaining squares, making six rows. Press seams towards sashing.

6. Sew a 39" sashing strip to the bottom of each of the six rows. Press seams toward the sashing strips.

7. Sew rows together. Press seams toward the sashing strips.

8. Sew the remaining 39" sashing strip to the top of the set of rows, pressing toward the sashing strip.

9. Sew the two 49½" sashing strips to the sides of the set of rows, pressing seams toward the sashing strips.

Border #1

1. Sew the 10" x 49½" border #1 strips to the sides of the quilt. Press seams toward the border. Sew the 10" x 60" border #1 strips to the top and bottom of the quilt.

2. Make hexies for border #1 from the 220 circles.

3. Arrange hexies on border #1 as shown in the quilt photograph. Pin in place and appliqué (by hand or machine) to the border.

Note: You may choose to hand stitch these hexies together before pinning and appliquéing them in place.

Border #2

1. Sew the 68½" border #2 strips to the sides of the quilt, pressing seams away from center of quilt.

2. Sew the 62" border #2 strips to the top and bottom of the quilt, pressing seams away from center of quilt.

Border #3

1. Sew the 70½" border #3 strips to the sides of the quilt, pressing seams away from center of quilt.

2. Sew the 70" border #3 strips to the top and bottom of the quilt, pressing seams away from center of quilt.

Quilt as desired.

COLOR EXPLOSION

COLOR EXPLOSION

Designed and made by Dr. Peggy G. Rhodes

Professionally Quilted by Elayne Vognild

Quilt size 45½" x 33½"

Skill Level: Advanced (or confident intermediate)

AccuQuilt® Die: 4" circle

Create your very own impressionistic watercolor masterpiece by using hexagons.

Though the use of hexagons is more difficult than most watercolor processes, the technique is still the same. Color saturation and depth is created through the strategic placement of colors according to light, medium, and dark values. Start with your own stash of colorful scraps and yardage and you may be able to design your work of art without purchasing anything new. Approximately 100 different fabrics were used to make the hexies for COLOR EXPLOSION.

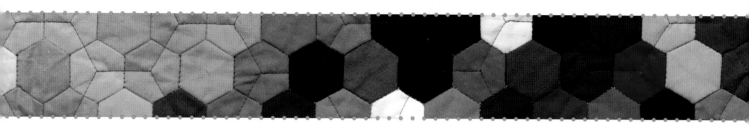

| Quilt size 45" x 49" | Fabric Credit: Kona® Cotton Solids by Robert Kaufman |
| Skill Level: Advanced | AccuQuilt® Die: 3" circle |

1. Select a photo (Fig. 82).

2. Use photo-editing software with a mosaic hexagon feature to manipulate the photo. There are many options available for different operating systems.

   You should end up with something like Figure 83.

3. Use a Kona® Cotton swatch chart (readily available to purchase) to select fabric colors to match (Fig. 84).

4. Cut lots of circles and make lots of hexies! Place each color family (grays, browns, rusts, etc.) in a small container.

5. Pick a place on the pattern to start—for Mickey, Julia started on one of his eyes. Pin hexies to a design wall, one at a time. Step away frequently to make sure the design is coming together.

6. Once all the hexies are pinned in place and you're satisfied with the results, hand stitch them together in rows. String one row at a time onto a needle and thread from left to right. The individual hexies in a row can then be sewn together one at a time without getting them out of order.

7. Hand stitch rows together.

8. Quilt as desired. In order to prevent tucks on the back of the quilt during the quilting process, use fusible web to fuse the backing to the batting before quilting. A heavy-duty needle, such as a top-stitch needle is also helpful.

Fig. 82

Fig. 83

Fig. 84

MOTHER'S FLOWERS

Designed and made by Dr. Peggy G. Rhodes
Background made by Virginia T. Bonham
Professionally quilted by Elayne Vognild

Quilt size 69" x 87"

Skill Level: Beginner - Advanced

AccuQuilt® Die: 4" circle

MOTHER'S FLOWERS

*Should you be lucky enough to inherit several completed hexagon flower units intended for a traditional Grandmother's Flower Garden quilt...*or if you began making flowers through one of the other methods but never finished enough for a quilt, you can combine what you have with hexies from circles and complete MOTHER'S FLOWERS in record time. Use the chart in the To The Rescue! section to determine the size circles needed in order to make hexagons the same size as what you have.

These new, easy to make hexies can be added to your existing flowers or used to create new flowers. Sixteen of the flowers used for this quilt were made using Brandy's Mylar templates while I sat at the hospital with my mother, who was in intensive care, for 27 days. Several years after she passed away, I learned to make flowers using circles of fabric instead of Mylar templates. I added to some I had started, made new ones, and then combined the old and the new to create this special contemporary flower garden in memory of my mother.

FABRIC REQUIREMENTS

Background
(can be cut from multiple scraps/fat quarters/yardage)
- Light Neutral –1½ yards
- Medium Neutral –1½ yards
- Dark Neutral –1½ yards

The neutrals could be pale blue or green instead of beige/tan. The important thing is to use neutrals that create interest and give the background texture without competing with the flowers and stems.

Flowers
(based on 25 flowers using 3½" to 4" circles)
- Yellow prints: scraps, fat quarters, or ⅛ yard cuts

- 25 "pairs" of coordinated floral prints (each pair has a matching or coordinated small print and large print or a pair with a solid and a print)—scraps, fat quarters or ⅛ yard cuts

Stems
½ yard of each of 5 different greens
Note: MOTHER'S FLOWERS could be made with only one green fabric for all the stems. If you choose to use only one green fabric, you will need about 1½ yards.

Borders and Binding
2½ yards

OTHER SUPPLIES

Spray starch (optional but helpful)

Open-toe foot for sewing machine

Neutral thread

Clear and smoke monofilament thread or thread to match your fabrics

Template or AccuQuilt® Die for the size circle(s) needed

Sandwich bags or clips

Fabric glue stick

FABRIC PREPARATION

1. If you think the colors in the fabric may bleed or fade, it is a good idea to pre-wash.

2. Before cutting, starch all of the fabric. You will have less raveling, the folds will be clean and crisp, the strips will be straighter, and the appliqué will have little to no puckering.

CUTTING DIRECTIONS

1. **Background**
Cut the light/medium/dark neutrals into 2½" strips from the width of fabric. You will need approximately 737" of light, medium, and dark neutral strips

The background could be made with scrappy squares and rectangles sewn together randomly. This method also produces the texture needed for the background.

2. **Flower Centers**
Cut 25 circles from the yellow print fabric. Unless you want all of your centers from the same fabric, use as many different yellows as you have available.

3. **Flower Petals**
After you've determined what size circle you need, cut six circles from each of the small print fabrics and 12 circles from each of the large print fabrics. Keep these 18 circles together in a set (small sandwich bags or clips work well for this). Feel free to "fussy cut" anything you want to be in the center of the hexie.

4. **Stems**
Fold the fabric on the diagonal to create a bias edge. Trim the bias fold and then cut five strips 3" and six strips 2½". This is more than you will need but it will allow you to audition the placement of various colors. If you want to use the exact placement as shown here, you will need the following amounts:

- **Green Fabric A**
  43" of 2½" strips and 159" of 3" strips
- **Green Fabric B**
  40" of 2½" strips and 169" of 3" strips
- **Green Fabric C**
  76" of 2½" strips and 156" of 3" strips
- **Green Fabric D**
  101" of 2½" strips and 161" of 3" strips
- **Green Fabric E**
  166" of 3" strips

5. **Borders**
Cut eight strips 8½" x width of fabric

6. **Binding**
Cut eight strips 2" width of fabric

INSTRUCTIONS

1. **Flowers**

   Follow the instructions in the Making Hexies section to make hexies from circles. Once the hexies are made, sew them into rows, and then into flowers as described in the Flower Units section.

   Even if you are joining the circle hexies to other hexagons made by another method, the procedure is the same. The flowers will look different on the back but you will not be able to tell the difference from the front (Fig. 85).

2. **Rail Fence neutral background**

   Sew the light strips to the medium strips and add the dark strips to the medium strips. Press the seams toward the darker strips. It is important for the design that the light strips are first, the medium strips are in the middle, and the dark strips are last. When sewn together, the three strips should equal 6½". If not, check the ¼" seam allowance and make the necessary adjustment.

3. Cut these neutral strip-sets into 6½" squares. You need a total of 108 blocks.

4. Sew the blocks together in a Rail Fence pattern. The width will be nine blocks across and the length will be 12 blocks. The first row begins with a horizontal strip block with the lightest neutral at the top. The second block is vertical with the lightest neutral first.

   Continue alternating the horizontal and vertical blocks in each row. All of the odd numbered rows will begin with a horizontal block and all the even rows will begin with a vertical block.

   Check the Rail Fence design by letting your eye follow the darkest strips. If they form a "zigzag" pattern, then the piecing is correct.

5. Join two of the border strips using a diagonal seam. Repeat three more times for the other three borders.

Fig. 85

6. Measure the pieced background to be sure it is square. If not, adjust some of the seams. You may also measure each side and the middle, divide by 3, and use this measurement to "square" the background. Whichever method you use, cut the left and right side borders the same length and attach them to the background. Press the seams toward the borders.

7. Measure across the top and bottom of the background (including the newly added side borders). Cut the top and bottom borders the same width. Attach the top border but wait until you've appliquéd the stems before you add the bottom border.

8. Join the 2½" strips for each of the green colors together with diagonal seams. If you do not want to have really long bias pieces of each color, you can use the measurements listed in #4 under Cutting Directions to make the stem lengths that you need.

Fig. 86

Fig. 87

9. Fold the strips in half with wrong sides of the fabric together. Sew narrow seams (just less than ¼") to make each of the strips a tube. Rotate the seam so that it is in the middle of the strip and press the seam open. Do this for each of the stems (Figs. 86–87).

10. Using the diagram (or creating your own pattern), lay out the stems on the quilt top (Fig. 88). Since I wanted some curves in the stems, I found it easier to lay the quilt on my cutting table rather than hanging it on the design wall. The letters below the stems in the diagram correspond to the green color in the cutting directions. The lower case letters represent the thinner green stems and the upper case letters designate the wider stems.

Note: Many of the stems cross other stems—it does not matter which ones are on top. Some of the stems split; make sure the unfinished end of the "off-shoot" stem is under the main stem. At least 1" of the stem tops should be under the flowers and it is okay if several inches are hidden under the flowers. It is helpful to lay the flowers on the stems to be sure you have the correct lengths and that the flowers do not overlap. If they do, shorten one of the stems so that each of the flowers can stand alone. When you are satisfied with the design, remove the flowers.

11. Insert a pencil or disappearing pen under the edge toward the middle of the stem and draw a line marking the stem's placement. Do this for each of the stems. Leave the stems in place as you complete the markings. The markings will be covered by the stems so they don't have to be perfect (Fig. 89).

12. Remove one stem at a time and trace the marking for that stem with the fabric glue.

    Replace the stem and press into place. Continue this process until all the stems are glued in place. The glue will temporarily hold the stems in place while you appliqué them. If you do not want to use the glue, pin the stems in place (Fig. 90).

13. Choose a matching thread or monofilament thread for the stem appliqué. The bobbin and top thread should be the same.

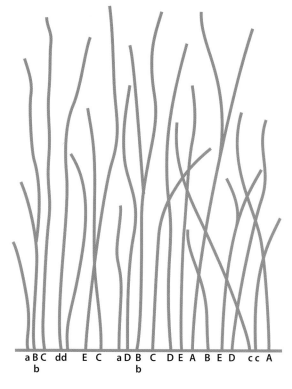

a B C   dd   E C   a D B   C   D E A   B E D   c c   A
  b   b

Fig. 88

14. Machine set-up for appliqué: Use a sharp 60/8 or 65/9 needle. Set your machine to the blind hem stitch (three or four straight stitches on the right and then a zigzag to the left) or a very narrow blanket stitch. The distance between the stitches to the left should be about ⅛" apart. Use an open-toe foot so that you can see the stitches. The straight stitches should be just off the edge of the stems. Check to be sure you do NOT have the single needle plate on your machine.

15. Appliqué the stems that go under other stems first. Lift the edges of the top stems and make a few stitches under the top stem. When the top stem is appliquéd, the bottom stitches will be locked in place.

16. Add the bottom border. Stretch the bottom of the background to fit the precut border. Even though the appliqué has "pulled in" the background, it can easily be pulled back into shape with the border.

17. Place the flowers at the ends of the stems, covering at least an inch of the stem—more is fine. Pin in place.

18. Either machine or hand appliqué the flowers in place. I hand appliquéd because I didn't want the stitches to show around the edges of the flowers but it is your choice.

19. Add batting and a backing and quilt as desired.

20. Square-up the quilt; add a sleeve (if desired) and bind.

Congratulations!
You have finished MOTHER'S FLOWERS.

Fig. 89

Fig. 90

Mama's Flowers

MAMA'S FLOWERS (46" x 60"), made by Dr. Peggy G. Rhodes, is a smaller version of MOTHER'S FLOWERS. It features a different color choice for the borders and is more heavily quilted.

The background was pieced by Virginia Tate Bonham (Warrior, AL) and it was professionally quilted by Judy Collins (Birmingham, AL).

To the Rescue!

Everything you need to know about Hexies

Hexie Reference Guide

Though the projects in this book are clear as to the size and number of hexies you will need, you may wish to:

- Change the size of the project;
- Use a different size circle of fabric; or
- Combine the circle hexies with hexies you already have.

When this occurs, refer to this reference section to answer your questions and assist you with planning your hexie project.

Size of Circle	Measurements of Folded Hexie			Number of Circles per Each Half Yard of Fabric
	Each Side	Point to Point	Straight Edge to Straight Edge	
14"	4"	8"	7"	3
13"	3¾"	7½" –	6½"	3
12"	3½"	6⅞" +	6"	3
11"	3⅛" +	6⅜"	5½"	3
10"	2⅞"	5¾"	5"	5
9"	2⅝"	5⅛"	4½"	8
8"	2¼" +	4½" +	4"	10
7"	2"	4"	3½"	10
6"	1¾"	3½" –	3"	18
5"	1⅜" +	2⅞"	2½"	24
4"	1⅛" +	2⅜" –	2"	40
(wide-mouth canning lid) 3⅜"	1"	1⅞" +	1⅝" +	44
3"	⅞"	1¾"	1½"	78
(regular canning lid) 2⅝"	¾" +	1½" +	1⅜"	90
2"	⅝"	1⅛" +	1"	180
1"	¼" +	⅝" –	½" –	720

The "+" or "-" that follows some of the measurements indicates that the actual measurement is a few threads over or under the measurement given.

How Many Hexies Do I Need?

There are many considerations in determining the number of hexies you will need to complete a project:

- If you are making the entire quilt with hexies, it will take a good many more than if you are going to appliqué them either individually or in groups/flowers onto the background of the quilt.

- The larger the hexie, the more space it will occupy. If you are making a large quilt of hexies sewn together then you will probably want to use the largest circles that your fabric will allow.

- What size quilt do you want to make?

The following chart will assist you in determining how many hexies you will need. There are several assumptions that were made as this table was developed.

- The quilt sizes are approximations based on the most common sizes for a throw, twin, full, queen, and king quilt.

- These sizes allow for the size of the mattress and an approximate 10" drop on three sides. A pillow tuck has not been included.

- The hexies are arranged in vertical rows and all odd-numbered rows will have one more hexie than even-numbered rows.

- The quilts start and end with an odd-numbered vertical row so that the four corners will match.

- The top and bottom of the quilts will have a straight edge by folding in half the hexies at the top and bottom of the odd-numbered rows. It is not recommended to cut these hexies in half unless you plan to stay stitch them on either side of the cut.

- The sides of the quilts will not be bound, maintaining the "zigzag" created by joining the hexies together.

- Since you will probably want to use scraps and/or combinations of multiple fabrics, the table shows you how many hexies of each size that you will be able to cut from a half yard of fabric.

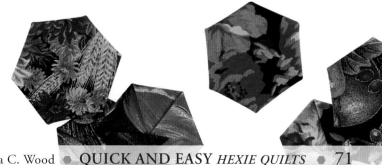

"HOW MANY HEXIES DO I NEED?" REFERENCE GUIDE

| Size | Approx. Dimensions | Circle Size | Number of Hexies Needed | Vertical Rows | | | | Number of Circles per Half Yard of Fabric |
| | | | | Odd Numbered | | Even Numbered | | |
				Rows	Hexies	Rows	Hexies	
Throw	44" x 56"	14"	60	4	9	3	8	3
	48⅜" x 60"	12"	95	5	11	4	10	3
	48⅞" x 60"	10"	138	6	13	5	12	5
	45" x 60"	8"	202	7	16	6	15	10
	45½" x 60"	6"	345	9	21	8	20	18
	44⅜" x 60"	4"	763	13	31	12	30	40
Twin	68" x 84"	14"	138	6	13	5	12	3
	69⅛" x 84"	12"	185	7	15	6	14	3
	66⅛" x 85"	10"	263	8	18	7	17	5
	65¼" x 84"	8"	409	10	22	9	21	10
	61¼" x 84"	6"	656	12	29	11	28	18
	61⅞" x 84"	4"	1,488	18	43	17	42	40
Full	80" x 84"	14"	163	7	13	6	12	3
	79½" x 84"	12"	218	8	15	7	14	3
	74¾" x 85"	10"	298	9	18	8	17	5
	78¾" x 84"	8"	495	12	22	11	21	10
	77" x 84"	6"	827	15	29	14	28	18
	75⅞" x 86"	4"	1,871	22	44	21	43	40
Queen	80" x 91"	14"	176	7	14	6	13	3
	79½" x 90"	12"	233	8	16	7	15	3
	83⅜" x 90"	10"	352	10	19	9	18	5
	85½" x 92"	8"	588	13	24	12	23	10
	82¼" x 90"	6"	946	16	31	15	30	18
	82⅞" x 90"	4"	2,139	24	46	23	45	40
King	104" x 91"	14"	230	9	14	8	13	3
	100¼" x 90"	12"	295	10	16	9	15	3
	100⅝" x 90"	10"	426	12	19	11	18	5
	99" x 92"	8"	682	15	24	14	23	10
	98" x 90"	6"	1,129	19	31	18	30	18
	100⅜" x 90"	4"	2,594	29	46	28	45	40

Width

Odd-numbered vertical rows are measured "Point to Point" and even-numbered vertical rows use the "Side" measurement to determine the width.

Divide the desired width by the sum of row 1 point to point and row 2 side measurements. This will give you the number of odd/even vertical rows you will need for the desired width. Since you want to end with the same kind of row you started with, add one more point to point measurement and increase the number of odd rows by one.

Length

The "straight edge to straight edge" measurement is used to determine the length.

Divide the desired length by the "straight edge to straight edge" measurement for the size circle that you are using. The answer will give you the number of hexies needed in each even numbered vertical row. If the answer does not yield a whole number, round up and the length will be a little larger than the original desired size. Remember that the odd-numbered rows will have one additional hexie in them but that will not change the length since the top and bottom hexies are folded to "match" the even rows.

Number of Hexies Needed

Once you know how many vertical rows you need and how many hexies are in each row, it is easy to calculate the total number of hexies you will need.

- Multiply the odd-numbered rows by the number of hexies in the row.

- Multiply the even-numbered rows by the number of hexies in the row (there will be one less row and one less hexie for the even vertical rows).

- **Add the two totals together for the total number of hexies needed.**

The reference guide provides the number of hexies you can usually get from a half yard of fabric. This may vary according to the width of the fabric and the accuracy of the half yard cut. Do not be alarmed by the amount of fabric you will need to complete a project. Depending on the size of your stash, you can probably use scraps or yardage you already have to complete most, if not all, of the project. And, it is your choice whether to add backing, batting, and additional quilting.

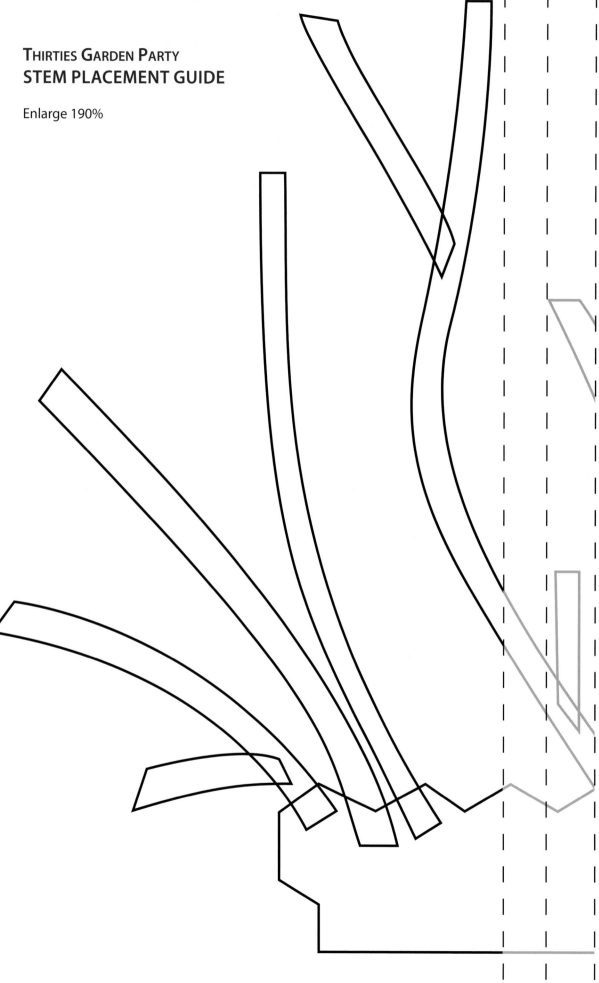

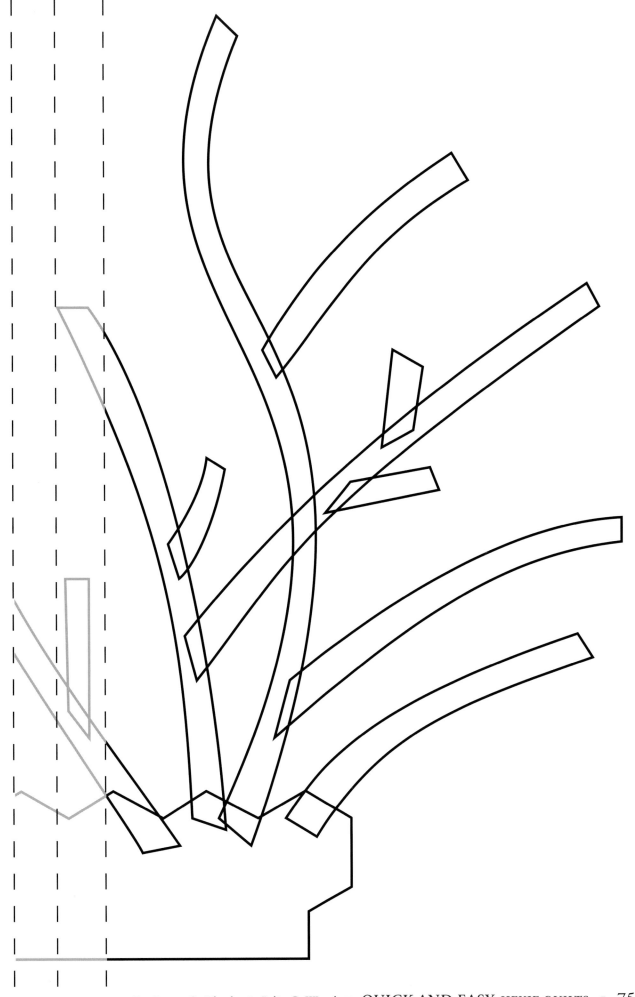

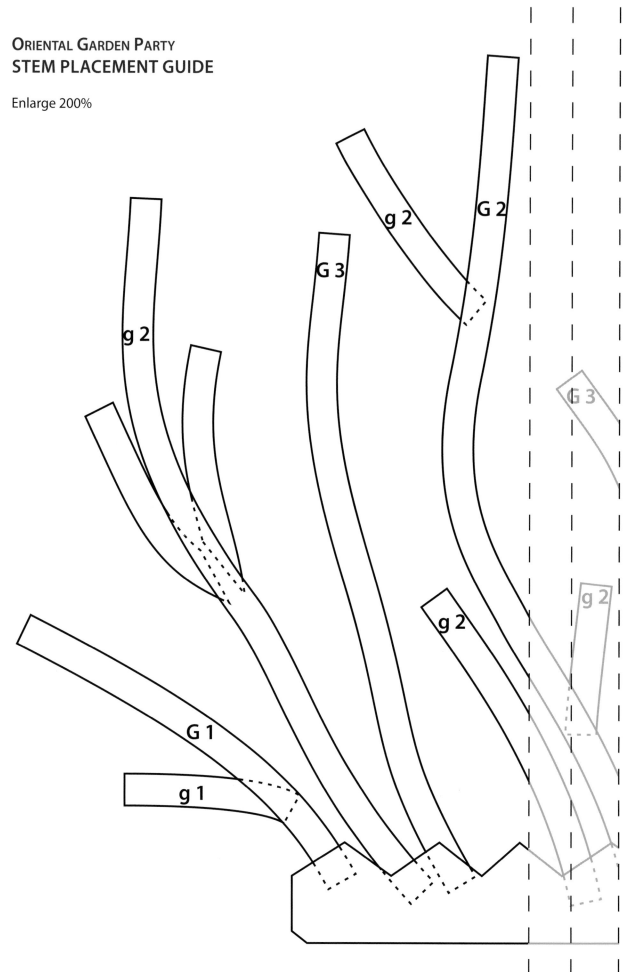

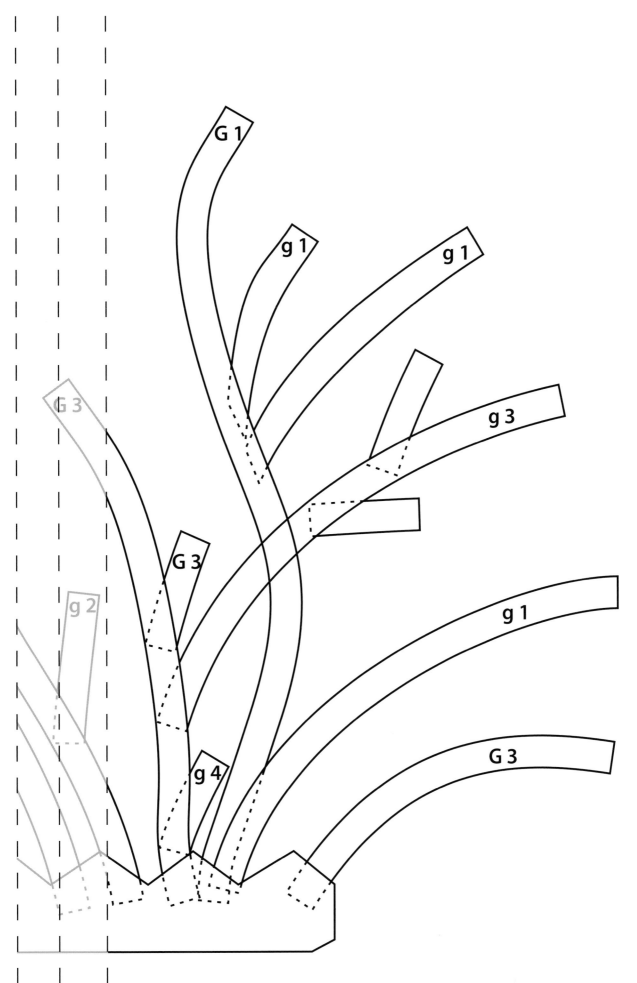

Hexagon Graph Paper *for* Designing

Copy this graph paper and use it to design your own hexie masterpiece!

About *the* Authors

Dr. Peggy G. Rhodes retired as Associate Dean from the University of Alabama's Continuing Education Program (UAB Special Studies) in 1993 and at the top of her "To Do" list was a return to quilting. Peggy sampled quilting for the first time as a child when she and her grandmother made a Bow Tie quilt totally by hand. Peggy still has the quilt, though it is literally falling apart. Peggy's love of learning new skills led to a return to teaching as she shared her techniques with friends, quilt shops and quilt guilds in Northwest Florida and Alabama. Her desire to learn more about quilting led her to the Birmingham Quilters Guild where she was able to expand her knowledge and explore new techniques through the national teachers' program.

Dr. Peggy G. Rhodes & Julia C. Wood

Peggy became interested in the Grandmother's Flower Garden block when she was looking for a project to work on while she sat at the hospital with her mother. That was in 2003 and she still loves to make hexies anytime she's waiting—doctors' offices, airports, riding in a car, watching TV, etc. In addition to this on-going project, she loves to explore quilting books and magazines to select new patterns. Selecting fabrics and completing the piecing of the blocks are her favorite parts of the quilting process.

Peggy lives with her husband, Ronald, in Warrior, Alabama, and in their spare time, they both enjoy fishing, cooking, and "front porch" style bluegrass music. In addition, Peggy has been planning and conducting workshops, seminars, conferences and retreats for the past 30+ years in areas such as strategic planning, team building, self-assessment, communication, individual and group goal-setting, and quilting (e.g., Wearables, Watercolor, Mariner's Compass, Quilt As You Go).

Contact: peggygrhodes@aol.com

Julia C. (Judy) Wood started sewing as a child, but her life took a more technical route during her career as an engineer. When she stopped working to stay at home with her children, Judy returned to her creative roots and began quilting. Her love of computer technology and quilting led to the development of her technique to create quilted portraits of people and pets, as demonstrated in her first book, *Fabric Photo Play*, AQS, 2005.

Judy has enjoyed teaching quilting nationally and locally for years, and gets tons of satisfaction from seeing students get excited about learning new techniques. She also has a popular quilting blog, greenquilts.blogspot.com, read regularly by hundreds of quilters. To celebrate the publication of her second book (and to celebrate the wonderful hexie!), Judy has established another blog: thehexieblog.blogspot.com. Be sure to check it out for lots of fun and inspirational hexie ideas!

When not quilting, Judy also enjoys cooking. She's been a two-time finalist in the Pillsbury Bake-Off. She also enjoys boating and relaxing at a nearby lake with her husband, Mark, and their two dogs. Her two daughters are now grown and love to be the recipients of their mom's quilts. Julia and Mark live in Auburn, Alabama.

Contact: juliacwood@mac.com
         greenquilts.blogspot.com
         thehexieblog.blogspot.com

More AQS books

This is only a small selection of the books available from the American Quilter's Society. AQS books are known worldwide for timely topics, clear writing, beautiful color photos, and accurate illustrations and patterns. The following books are available from your local bookseller, quilt shop, or public library.

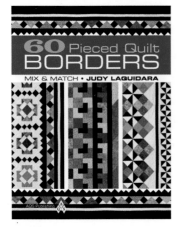

#8662 .... $26.95

#1245 .... $19.95

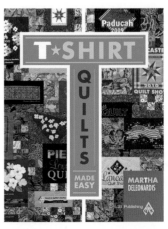

#8664 .... $19.95

#8671 .... $24.95

#8146 .... $26.95

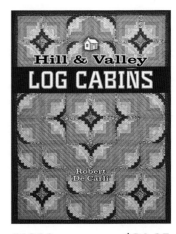

#1246 .... $24.95

#1249 .... $24.95

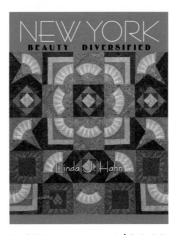

#1251 .... $24.95

#8532 .... $26.95

LOOK for these books nationally.
CALL or **VISIT** our website at

1-800-626-5420
www.AmericanQuilter.com